"Nobody, but nobody can make it out here alone."

— Maya Angelou

Praise for *Positive Influence*

"I just finished reading this remarkable new book. The Parker's have tackled the very complex concept of positive influence as a critical leadership competency in a very compelling way. They not only present real-life stories of positive influence, but they offer the reader a means of assessing and managing their influence style. I offer the book and its authors my highest endorsement. Well done!"

Richard Kropp, Vice President and Chief Human Resources Officer MorseLife Health System and author, *Communicating in the Business Environment*

"With captivating stories, thought-provoking questions and practical techniques, *Positive Influence* paints a vibrant, memorable portrait of what it means to be a profound leader who inspires and enriches the lives of others."

Chip R. Bell, author, *Managers as Mentors*

"Positive leaders are one in a hundred. However, if you are truly committed to becoming a leader who is a positive influence on people, this is a must-read. Using insights gained from a series of in-depth interviews with a wide variety of leaders, the Parkers expose us to leadership excellence and provide a roadmap to becoming a positive and effective leader."

Robert E Quinn, Professor, Center for Positive Organizations, University of Michigan, Ross School of Business, and author, *The Positive Organization* and co-author, *The Economics of Higher Purpose*

"If, like me, you've ever had someone say, 'I'm here for you,' and then follow it up with action, the stories and action steps in *Positive Influence* will resonate with you. No one is an island, and this book from Michael and Glenn Parker reminds us all of the role we play in the lives of those around us—at home, at work, and in the world."

Robert Hoffman, Global Head, Organizational Development Novartis Global Drug Development and co-author, *Meeting Excellence: 33 Tools to Lead Meetings That Get Results*

"Glenn Parker is an old friend of mine, and he has written a very useful book with his son that reframes leadership, which is much needed in this day and age. We need better leadership. We need more positive and life affirming leadership. And we need it to come from all of us. Michael and Glenn offer us a very useful path in this direction."

Peter Block, author of *Flawless Consulting* and *The Empowered Manager* and founder of Designed Learning

"We are in a relationship and connection economy where leadership is defined as the ability to influence individual gifts towards shared goals. That's why this book is a goldmine for leaders. It shows how to individualize leadership for different types of people, balance self-fulfillment with service to others, and transform negative drain into positive potential. Most importantly, The Positive Influence Leader reminds leaders that we are in this together."

Nate Regier, author *of Beyond Drama, Conflict Without Casualties*, and coming up...*Seeing People Through*.

Table of Contents

Preface vii

PART 1 LEAN ON ME

1 You Didn't Build that Alone 1

2 Discovering the Dimensions of Positive Influence Leadership 3

PART 2 THE FOUR TYPES OF POSITIVE INFLUENCE LEADERS

3 The Supportive Leader 23

4 The Teacher Leader 33

5 The Motivating Leader 43

6 The Role Model Leader 55

PART 3 HELPING PEOPLE BECOME THEIR BEST SELF

7 Profile of the Positive Influence Leader 69

8 Pay It Forward: Be of Service to Others 81

9 Turning a Negative Influence into a Positive Force 91

10 The Positive Influence Leader in Times of Crisis 101

PART 4 TOOLS FOR THE POSITIVE INFLUENCE LEADER

The Parker Positive Influence Leader Survey: A Self-Assessment 119

Understanding Your Results 125

Tools for Becoming a More Effective Positive Influence Leader 126

My Improvement Plan 127

References 129

Preface

An email popped up in Glenn's inbox one morning informing him that Bill had passed away and a memorial would be held on Sunday. Bill was a long-time client who had morphed into a good friend over the years. After coming to terms with the news, Glenn began to reflect on the years with Bill, especially his impact on Glenn's growth and development.

Bill had engaged Glenn as a team-building consultant to create a series of problem-solving teams around the division. After the teams were up and running, Bill asked that Glenn develop a customer service training program for all employees. When Glenn hesitated and said, "I really have no experience," Bill's reply was simply "You'll learn." Later, Bill said corporate has a mandatory business ethics training course, but "I want a program tailored to our culture." Again, when Glenn hesitated, Bill replied, "You'll learn." There are other examples, but upon reflection, it was clear, as Glenn later said to Michael, "Bill was a significant positive influence on my career."

Michael pointed out a number of similar people in his life who were positive influences for him. Out of this discussion came the genesis of this book as both Michael and Glenn agreed that there must be many other people out there who can say with confidence that "without this person I would not be where I am today."

Background and Purpose of the Book

We began our research with the goal of creating a profile of the positive influence leader. We wanted to build the profile with a "bottoms-up" approach. While we began with an overarching goal, our methodology was such that we were open to allowing the data to "speak to us." In other words, we would remain open and flexible and thus allow the data to shape our thinking and, therefore, our conclusions.

The data would be in the form of quotes and insights from a series of interviews with leaders doing a variety of jobs across a broad spectrum of industries and organizations. Industries represented among the people in our interview group are financial services, pharmaceutical, healthcare, government, consulting, non-profit, and manufacturing. Among the 50 or so people in the group are an almost equal number of men and women, a variety of ethnic groups, as well as people born in countries such as

Peru, South Korea, Taiwan, Spain, and Mexico in addition to the United States. For the most part, interviewees are college educated, and many hold advanced degrees as well.

Interviews were mainly conducted by phone, although some were done in-person. All interviews used the same interview guide. The guide, sent to interviewees prior to the interview, included five open-ended questions:

1. What people in your work or personal life have had a positive influence on you?
2. Let's talk about one (or more) of these people who had a positive influence on you. Tell me how and in what ways they were a positive influence on you.
3. Now, let's talk about some of the principles that you learned from this person that you incorporate in your work or personal life today.
4. Take a moment to think about a person upon whom you have had a positive influence. If asked, what do you think they would say that you did that had a positive impact on them?
5. Have you ever encountered a negative influence person—someone who was not supportive or did not think you could do something—who directly or indirectly discouraged you? And did you use that lack of support as motivation to prove them wrong and turn that negative into a source of positive influence?

It is important to note that we added question 5 after a number of people told us about a person who tried to be a negative influence on them. They also told us how they handled the negative talk. As we indicated earlier, we allowed the data "to speak to us." In this case, enough people told us about negativity and its potential impact that we felt it was important to add it to our interview guide. We also went back and asked people we had interviewed earlier in the process if they ever encountered a negative influence person and how they handled it.

Over time, what emerged from the data set was not a single profile of a positive influence leader, but rather four different types or styles of positive influence leader. We found that a person can be a positive influence on others in ways that are different from other positive influence leaders.

For example, some leaders make it clear they are backing you and will support your efforts to achieve your goals while others teach you things you need to learn in order to be successful. While different, both can be helpful, especially when they are targeted to your specific needs at the very time you need them. Again, the data spoke, and we listened as people told us stories of their interactions with positive influence leaders.

In the final analysis, the book is both inspirational and instructive. We hope that you are moved to become a positive influence leader or learn ways to increase your current effectiveness as a positive influence leader. We believe the stories that emerged from the interviews about how positive influence leaders altered the lives and careers of people will motivate you to action. If you are moved to take action, the book provides suggestions and tools to support your efforts.

Audiences

We wrote the book with a number of people in mind:

- Senior-level leaders in the private, public, and nonprofit sectors who want to create a positive influence culture in their organization.
- Managers and supervisors who want to be positive influence leaders or who want to increase their effectiveness as a positive influence leader.
- Human resources professionals who are looking for ways to improve their performance management and reward systems to emphasize positive influence as a factor in their systems.
- Learning and talent-development professionals who want to create employee development programs that help people become positive influence leaders.
- Professionals in a variety of organizations who want to expand their repertoire to include being a positive influence on others.
- Project managers and team leaders who want to bolster their team's confidence so that they can accomplish the team's goal and encourage members of the team to be a positive influence on other members of the team.

Overview of the Contents

Positive Influence has four parts: *Lean on Me, The Four Types of Positive Influence Leaders, Helping People Become Their Best Self, and Tools for Becoming a Positive Influence Leader*. In addition, at the end of each chapter there is a section called *Looking Back: Some Issues to Consider*. Here, in addition to providing some summary comments, we provide four discussion questions that are intended to help you reflect on and absorb the key points of the chapter.

In *Lean on Me,* specifically in Chapter One, *You Didn't Build That Alone*, we provide examples from our work life and those of well-known people that introduce the idea of positive influence leadership. We also dispel the myth of the rugged individualist as we show that most people, even famous people, have some help along the way.

Chapter Two, *Discovering the Dimensions of Positive Influence Leadership,* introduces our central thesis that effective leaders are a positive influence on the members of their team, but their impact may be achieved in different ways. Some are supportive, some are teachers, some are motivators, and some are role models. The transformational leader, however, is situational. She can provide just what you need at the very time you need it. We introduce and briefly describe the four types of positive influence leader: the supportive leader, the teacher leader, the motivating leader, and the role model leader.

In Part Two we describe *The Four Types of Positive Influence Leaders* using multiple examples from our interview group. Chapter Three defines *The Supportive Leader*, Chapter Four *The Teacher Leader*, Chapter Five *The Motivating Leade*r, and Chapter Six describes *The Role Model Leader*.

Part Three focuses on *Helping People Become Their Best Self*. Chapter 7, *Profile of the Positive Influence Leader*, lays out the four styles in detail and in all their many variations. Chapter 8, *Pay it Forward: Be of Service to Others*, provides many examples from our interviews of the ways people who benefitted from a positive influence leader in their lives have been, in turn, a positive influence on others. Chapter 9, *Turning a Negative Influence into a Positive Force*, focuses on the experiences of a variety of people who were subjected to a negative person and the various strategies they used to deal with the negativity and go on to succeed in life. The final chapter of Part Three, Chapter 10, *The Positive*

Influence Leader in Times of Crisis, describes the characteristics of a positive influence leader and the variety of ways they lead in times of crises.

Part Four, *Tools for the Positive Influence Leader*, answers the question "So what?" Here is where you will find the means to apply the learnings from the book. First, you will have an opportunity to complete and score *The Parker Positive Influence Leader Survey.* Then there is guide to *Understanding Your Results* that will help you interpret your scores. In *Tools for Becoming a More Effective Positive Influence Leader,* we provide a guide to the various ways you can use the survey data to your advantage. And finally, *My Improvement Plan* is a template for exactly that—creating your plan for become a more effective positive influence leader.

Acknowledgements

We want to thank all of the people who gave freely of their time to share their personal stories of positive influence during the course of the many interviews that give this book its unique flavor. You will see their names associated with the many quotes that are sprinkled throughout this book.

We also acknowledge our spouses, Marla and Judy, who are a positive influence on us in so many ways. Specifically, they supported the idea of the book, encouraged us to pursue the research, read parts of the manuscript, and provided helpful advice.

The Authors

Michael Parker is a senior executive with 25 years of experience and success in financial services. His areas of expertise include strategic growth, business development, relationship management, marketing, and public relations.

Currently, Michael is Managing Director with Rockefeller Capital Management.

Michael previously served as strategic advisor at HighTower Advisors, where he helped the company set and execute its strategic growth plans, and as executive vice president and chief development officer, with responsibility for driving revenue growth. He led the firm to a Top 5 ranking for six consecutive years and listing in the *Inc. Magazine* 5000 fastest-growth companies for five consecutive years.

Michael has also served as a vice president of business development at LPL Financial and as financial advisor and senior vice president of wealth management with Citi Group/Smith Barney.

Michael is a featured writer for *wealthmanagement.com,* where he has authored more than a dozen articles including: *What Did You Learn? On Wealth Management Leadership*; *The Right People with The Right Stuff*; *What Gets Measured, What Gets Done*; *Are You Willing to Sacrifice Growth?; Be the Buyer; Why You?*; *It's the Culture, Stupid*; and *Scrap the Strategic Planning Meetings, Just Tell a Great Story.*

In 2015, Michael created and authored *Blueprint for Growth*, an industry award-winning practice management program recognized by wealth-management.com.

Glenn Parker is a team building and organizational development consultant to many of the world's leading corporations, including Novartis, Merck, Lucent, and Accenture, as well as smaller businesses and government agencies. Glenn is the author of 15 business books, including the best-sellers, *Team Players and Teamwork: New Strategies for Developing Successful Collaboration* (John Wiley, 2008) and *Cross-Functional Teams: Working with Allies, Enemies and Other Strangers* (John Wiley, 2003). Glenn's assessment survey, the *Parker Team Player Survey* published by CPP, has sold more than one million copies.

Glenn has helped develop more than 20 learning programs for Accenture Academy in leadership and professional development, including a recent webinar on *Positive Influence*: *Finding People Who Can Help You Be Your Best Self*.

In his spare time, Glenn volunteers with the American Cancer Society where, 17 years ago, he co-founded *Run for Dad*, a Father's Day event that educates men about the dangers of prostate cancer, regularly draws some 1,500 people, and raises about $125,000 for cancer research.

Parker holds a BA from City College of New York, a master's from the University of Illinois and has studied for the doctorate at Cornell University. He also studied economic development at the University of Oslo, Norway.

Part 1

Lean on Me

Chapter 1
You Didn't Build That Alone

The performance evaluation meeting with my boss is going well. Then he says, "Let's talk about your development plan and what you want to do over the next year to improve." I should tell you that it's my first job out of grad school and this is my first performance assessment. My job involves doing research and writing reports. The work is repetitive and boring. On the other hand, to a 23-year old like me, the people over in education seem to be having lots of fun flying all over the country conducting leadership classes.

I ask my boss if I can observe a leadership class as part of my development. He responds, "As a matter of fact, I am travelling down South next week to run some workshops. And, Glenn, I'm happy to have you come with me, but I can't justify your travel expenses unless you conduct one of the classes." I panic and say, "Larry, what would I teach? I don't know anything." He tells me not to worry, he will figure out something I can do. And he was right. I was able to teach something useful, and the response was very positive. From that experience, I realized learning and development was my true north.

It was only many years later that I came to understand what Larry had done. He saw something in me—he believed in me, believed that I could teach and do it well. And rather than give me a rah-rah motivation talk, he created a situation and the conditions for me to be successful and realize it for myself. He was the first positive influence in my work life.

— Glenn

My first job managing people seemed to be going really well. I was working as a protégé to the one of the firm's top market managers in the country. Looking back, I might have started to falsely interpret his success as mine when I probably had little to do with any of it. Then one day, as we were getting dressed in the locker room after a workout discussing a job opportunity for me in another market, my boss turned to me and asked, "You know what I have noticed about you? You never seem to finish 100 percent of the job. You are always looking for the exit door before you can actually measure your contribution. Why is that?" No one had ever been so direct and so honest with me about how they really saw me. I needed the truth and my boss gave it to me. It hurt but it changed my life.

At that time, I was a sales manager for large firm in one of the most successful and profitable markets in the country. I really had no idea what I was doing, but my boss saw something in me and decided to take a risk that he did not need to take and invest in my development. We are still good friends today, and he continues to be one of my mentors and most significant influences.

After that awkward but necessary moment in the gym, I decided that he was giving me a gift by allowing me to simply observe how he worked in all aspects of leading and managing people. He had a gift for influencing the behavior of his salespeople and he knew how to find the right balance between being firm on the issues and soft on the people. Everyone knew he had their back. As a result, he was able to demand excellence from everyone. No one was exempt from delivering results, but they knew he cared about them and would do whatever his people needed to succeed. I never had to ask to be included in his phone calls or meetings. He insisted upon it and afterward he would ask, "What did you learn?" He would ask my opinion of how I thought he did because he had enough humility to always look for opportunities to grow and learn.

In my next role and every opportunity since that time, I have deployed many of the lessons and techniques he taught me. Those lessons have had enduring application. He saw something in me, but because I was so green, he decided to teach by example not by

> *letting me go off and try things on my own. I was not ready for that approach at the time and he knew it. Once I moved on to my next challenge, I was ready because of what he taught me.*
>
> *In my next role and every opportunity since that time, I have deployed many of the lessons and techniques he taught me. Those lessons have had enduring application. He saw something in me, but because I was so green, he decided to teach by example not by letting me go off and try things on my own. I was not ready for that approach at the time and he knew it. Once I moved on to my next challenge, I was ready because of what he taught me.*
>
> *He was not an energetic or enthusiastic leader, but he had presence like no one I have ever met. He did not make people feel warm. He made them feel safe, confident, trusted, and respected. Everyone respected and admired him...They still do.*
>
> — Mike

Lean on Me

At a campaign stop in Roanoke, Virginia, in 2012, President Obama got into some trouble for using the phrase "You didn't build that." He was making the point that many successful people and businesses owe their success, in part, to someone who helped along the way, as well as to the government that invested in roads and bridges and other types of business support, such as guaranteed loans. If the president had simply finished the sentence by saying, "You didn't build that alone," it would have been much clearer and more widely accepted since most successful entrepreneurs and business owners have some help along the way from either a teacher, mentor, partner, or friend. Steve Jobs acknowledges the influence and importance of Steve Wozniak and Steve Lasseter to the success of Apple and Pixar. Bill Gates and Paul Allen gratefully acknowledge the influence of Ed Roberts, the developer of an early personal computer. Joe Lacob could not have engineered the turnaround of the NBA's Golden State Warriors into the league's elite team without Peter Guber and other Silicon Valley investors who provided not only funding but advice on areas such as real estate and marketing.

Kareem Abdul-Jabbar is remembered by most as one of the greatest basketball players of all time. What many of us do not know is that Kareem's (his name was Lew Alcindor at the time) decision to attend UCLA to play for Coach John Wooden when he had his pick of colleges was one of the most important decisions of his life. It was Coach Wooden's influence that shaped the way Kareem lives his life today. In Kareem's recent book, *Coach Wooden and Me,* Kareem writes, "It is the realization that some lives are so extraordinary that their story must be told to generations to come so those values aren't diminished or lost altogether." The book tells us that:

> *Their relationship grew over a 50-year period. Wooden was both a teacher and an emotional guide to Kareem. Kareem could not have perfected his patented sky hook without Wooden relentlessly working him in practice, repeating shot after shot until Kareem got it right. There were no shortcuts. Wooden coached the team to three consecutive national titles with Kareem. Wooden and Kareem remained very close until Wooden's death in 2010.*

Our research indicates that you don't have to be famous or wildly successful to have benefitted from an influential person in your life. You don't get to be a highly regarded schoolteacher, doctor, corporate manager, or fitness instructor without some help along the way. Every person we interviewed had no problem identifying a person, often more than one, without whom they would not have made it.

The Myth of the Rugged Individualist

When you think of the Old West, perhaps you conjure up an image of a lone cowboy on his horse riding across the prairie. You may even see John Wayne or Gary Cooper as the strong and silent cowboy out there, just him and his horse. It was assumed that in order to be successful as a cowboy, a rancher, or farmer, you had to be self-reliant and independent because you were on your own. If you came West for a better life, you had to work hard because no one was going to help you.

Not true. For example, a single man could not operate a farm or ranch alone. He needed the help of a hard-working wife and many children. So it was that families working together contributed to the success of the family farm. Beyond that, communities of farmers often came together to help each other out with barn raising, building a school or church, fighting a fire on a neighbor's property, or collaborating on a potluck dinner or a community social. The federal government helped, too, providing land to settlers under the Homestead Act and supporting the construction of the first transcontinental railroad. Even in the Old West people did not do it alone.

Most 19th-century entrepreneurs who developed Western mining, agricultural, and railroad empires lauded themselves as rugged individualists who strongly opposed government regulation of wages, hours, and working conditions while, at the same time, lobbying for government subsidies and tariffs to protect their products from foreign imports. They wanted to be free to establish monopolies that often stifled competition and increased prices to consumers. These entrepreneurs may have launched their businesses by themselves, but they did not build their businesses alone. In addition to the government, they had a team of managers, supervisors, and workers who came together to create and grow the business.

And that collaborative tradition continues to this day. Talk to any 21st century entrepreneur and you will hear her say, "I have a great team, and we are successful because of them."

For example, Danny, one of the people we interviewed, said he could not have built his professional practice without his former boss and mentor, Susan, who trained him during his formative years. He also appreciates all the help he received from many of his clients who helped him shape his practice along the way.

A Hand Up, Not a Handout

No one can do it for you, but you don't have to do it alone. If you are fortunate, there are people along the way who provide the help you need when you need it. Supreme Court Justice Thurgood Marshall famously said,

> *None of us got where we are solely by pulling ourselves up by our bootstraps. We got here because somebody—a parent, a teacher, an Ivy League crony, or a few nuns—bent down and helped us pick up our boots.*

Interestingly, we have come to understand that a person may be positively influenced by someone even without having met them. Such a positive influence leader is almost always an iconic role model such as Ronald Reagan for a generation of politicians and Marlon Brando for several generations of actors.

Our research clearly shows that many people have been influenced by a teacher, a manager, or a parent who said, "You can do it" or "I will help you get through it." Call it a mentor, a coach, or simply a friend, someone was there for you at a critical juncture in your life. For example, Oprah Winfrey cites author and poet Maya Angelou as a special person who provided guidance through some of the most critical periods in her life.

Leslie, one of the people in our study group, after a number of years in the workforce, went back to graduate school to become a teacher. She was fortunate to encounter a professor who instilled in her a passion for teaching. He taught her all the practical tools she needed to be successful in the classroom, but he didn't map out a plan for her. And successful she was—so much so that in 2017 she was one of only nineteen people in the entire New York City School System to be selected as Teacher of the Year.

Stuart, a former senior-level executive at ADP, decided after many years of building a very successful 750M business to become an executive coach and team consultant for senior and executive leadership teams. He knew very little about his new direction, so he started by attending a Tony Robbins' seminar, "Unleash the Power Within," to get his mind in the right place. He sat up close to the stage because he figured that is where all of the other successful people would sit. Up in the front he met Jack, a long-time, very successful consultant practicing a very similar craft Stuart intended to pursue. Jack invited Stuart out to the West Coast to shadow Jack for a few days, which Stuart gladly did. Every moment on this trip was an opportunity to learn, and every interaction had a message. During their last day together, Jack slid a white envelope over to Stuart and inside was an invoice from Jack to Stuart in exchange for allowing Stuart to shadow him. Stuart told us:

> *Jack asked me, "Are you ready to do this?" Stuart gave Jack an affirmative response to which Jack replied, "When you pay me this invoice, that is when you know you are ready." Jack's point was, there are people like me who will help you, but they will not do it for you.*

Dr. Benjamin Mays, former president of Morehouse College, met Dr. Martin Luther King when he was an undergraduate at Morehouse, and the two remained close until Dr. King passed away in 1968. In his speeches and writings, Dr. King's emphasis on the dignity of all human beings and the failure of America to live up to its stated ideals came from Dr. Mays.

Frank, an IT manager we interviewed, coached a member of his team to handle user complaints without getting defensive. Frank told us, "I didn't intervene with the users; rather, I let him learn by handling it himself."

Hall of Fame basketball player Bill Russell said his mother was a great mentor. "She taught me to stand up for myself, to use my brainpower on my behalf." Although his mother died when he was 12, her influence stayed with him throughout his life, influencing his thoughts, goals, and aspirations. Russell's life is replete with examples of independent thinking and standing up for his beliefs.

In all of these cases, and in many others, the person was not handed a business or a job or a part in a movie. The gift they received was a "hand up"—an inspiring or supportive message from an influential person. That leader, mentor, teacher, coach, or parent was a positive influence on them such that they credit their success to that relationship. It is their strongly held belief that:

"Without this person, I would not be where I am today."

Looking Back: Some Issues to Consider

As our research has proceeded, we have found that many successful people have benefitted from multiple positive influence leaders over the course of their life and career. Growing up, that positive influence might have been a parent, a coach, or teacher; however, as they matured and entered the world of work they encountered a workplace leader who motivated them to chart a different path or found a role model who served as a positive influence example from whom they could learn what it takes to be successful.

We have discovered that positive influence leadership comes in a variety of forms, all of which can help you find success. In the next chapter we will begin to explore the different ways you can become or perhaps increase your effectiveness as a positive influence leader.

Positive Influence

1. Why were so many people, especially business people, upset with President Obama's phrase "You didn't build that"?
2. We say that the rugged individualist is a myth. However, do you know of some people who did, in fact, become very successful without any help along the way?
3. How do you feel about the line "No one can do it for you, but you don't have to do it alone"? Would you prefer to do it alone?
4. As a leader, how do you provide someone with a hand up while ensuring it is not a handout? Describe how you would handle that in a workplace situation.

Chapter 2
Discovering the Dimensions of Positive Influence

*Sometimes a positive influence in your life is a person who provides just the right amount of inspiration or motivation at just the right time in your life. Something she does or something she says that resonates with you that either gets you through a tough challenge or pushes you to achieve an elusive goal. For Erin, that person was Robin Roberts, co-host of ABC's Good Morning America. Roberts, a breast cancer survivor, was a difference-maker for Erin while she was going through her treatment for breast cancer. Erin told us, "It made a difference seeing her (Roberts) looking healthy, just doing her job, talking about everything except cancer. It helped me get through it knowing there is a life after this." In a postscript to this story, years later, Erin was walking in New York City and passed Roberts on the street. While Roberts was waiting for the light to change so she could cross the street, Erin got up the nerve to approach her. Erin told her how much of a positive influence Roberts was during the time of her treatment. Roberts removed her sunglasses and said "thank you for sharing your story with me," and gave Erin a big hug.**

Initially, we expected to find a set of characteristics or traits that hung together to form an effective positive influence leader. However, as we have discovered from both our research and our personal experience, successful positive influence leaders come in different sizes and shapes. In other words, one size does not fit all.

The Positive Influence Leader

A positive influence leader in your work life is often very supportive, frequently an exceptional teacher, at times quite motivating, and often, a confident role model. We introduce the four leader styles here and then explore each in some depth in subsequent chapters. Our thesis is that

*Interview with the author

effective and successful leaders all have a positive influence on the members of their team but in different ways and often with a different emphasis. In other words, you can be a highly successful leader using one or perhaps two of the four styles.

The Transformational Leader

The transformational positive influence leader is equally comfortable and skilled at using any one of the four styles. In addition, he is able to assess your needs at the moment and effortlessly alter his approach to provide just what you need at the very time you need it. In other words, he is situational.

Four Types of Positive Influence Leaders

We have identified four types or styles of positive influence leaders. The four types are:

- The Supportive Positive Influence Leader
- The Teacher Positive Influence Leader
- The Motivating Positive Influence Leader
- The Role Model Positive Influence Leader

Our research shows that all of us have the capacity to use the strengths of all four styles; we just happen to use one or perhaps two styles most often. For example, from our interviews we learned that certain leaders have been, at times, an effective teacher, while at other times they have provided a motivating type of leadership influence depending upon what the person needed at a specific time in their work life. Other combinations have emerged as well.

Personalize the Experience

As you review the description of the four styles, personalize the experience by analyzing the extent to which the description is aligned with your understanding of how you influence the people that you lead in the workplace.

The Supportive Positive Influence Leader

For many people, the first positive influence in their life was a parent or a grandparent who believed in them, encouraged them and supported them from their very first days. It is this capacity for being supportive that is one of the strengths of an effective leader. This ability to be supportive is usually learned early in life from a parent or grandparent.

Founder of the *Huffington Post*, Arianna Huffington grew up in a one-bedroom apartment in Athens, Greece. She credits her mother with being the most positive influence in her life. Huffington says:

> She made me feel that I could aim for the stars. And if I failed along the way, that is okay. Failure is not the opposite of success, she used to say, it's a stepping stone to success.

Actor and director Clint Eastwood says his mentor was his grandmother who encouraged him to pursue his dreams and "always thought I was going to be something when nobody else, including myself, thought I was going to amount to anything."

Gerald, an operations management consultant, who we interviewed, pointed to both his parents as being significant influences in his life but in different ways. He told us they were a strong motivating influence for his success throughout K-12, college, and later in the corporate world. At a young age, his father taught him how to do technical things such as use a slide rule and drafting scale while his mother helped instill a need for reading and writing communications. Both parents always challenged and believed in him. They both fully expected him to go to college, graduate, and be successful.

Adriana, a person in our study group, is a young female executive who came to the United States from Mexico to attend college and to pursue her career in business. She spoke of the example her parents set for she and her siblings. Adriana told us:

> My parents are the best example of how a marriage works, genuine care, affectionate, invested in their relationship to be better people for each other, their family and all other people around them. My mom's quiet strength drove their marriage and our family forward.

In 2014, during his MVP acceptance speech, basketball great Kevin Durant thanked his mother by saying:

> You are the real MVP. The odds were stacked against us. You made us believe. You kept us off the street. You put clothes on

our backs, food on our table. When you didn't eat, you made sure we ate. You sacrificed for us.

The Essence of the Supportive Positive Influence Leader

The supportive leader believes in her people, but more importantly, helps the members of her team believe in themselves. For example, Kevin Durant plays the game today like he is thanking his mother every time he plays.

The Teacher Positive Influence Leader

Many people point to that special teacher who inspired them to achieve greatness while teaching them important career skills and how to navigate bumps in the road of life.

Renowned CBS anchorman Walter Cronkite found his calling at age 16, thanks to Fred Birney, a journalism instructor whose classes led Cronkite to take an interest in journalism. Birney appointed Cronkite editor of the school newspaper and then, in 1933, secured a job for him as the *Houston Post's* correspondent at the University of Texas in Austin. As Cronkite later said, "Things would have been a lot different for me were it not for Fred Birney."

In a similar vein, physicist and astronaut Sally Ride, the first American woman to walk in space, credits her graduate school professor, Dr. Arthur Walker, for instilling confidence in her such that she believed she could accomplish anything she set her sights, even becoming an astronaut.

Glenn's mother was a teacher and the first and perhaps most influential person in his life. She was a kindergarten teacher and, since she was the only one in the school, she was also his kindergarten teacher. So, for that year, Glenn's teacher was also his mother, and, while he did not realize it at the time, she was the first great influence in his life. As he said, "She instilled in me a love of learning, especially the importance of reading."

Dave, a former CEO of a public company, talked about a college football coach who pulled him aside one day after practice and told him, "David, I believe you are capable of far more than you are giving." As a former high school All-American and highly recruited athlete, Dave at first thought his coach's feedback was misguided because no one had ever said anything like that to him. Dave realized that his college coach was the first one who had the courage to tell him the truth about what he saw. His coach did that because as Dave said:

> He saw something in me, something I did not even see in myself and it was a simple thing... I was capable of being far more that I was showing by simply coming to practice every day and giving my very best.

Dave told us no other coach had ever challenged him to be his very best and he wished they had. Dave's coach helped him recognize that the only way to reach his potential was to give maximum effort every day. After college in Dave's professional life he carried this mantra with him and lived by it for his entire career, becoming a highly successful CEO, author, and teacher.

For many women who grew up in an earlier time, a positive influence helped them tackle a job that was previously considered the sole purview of men. For example, Betsy, a woman we interviewed for the book, said her theater teacher convinced her that a woman could be successful working on the technical side of theater, such as building a set and lighting the stage.

Being an Effective Positive Influence Teacher

Teachers are great leaders when they teach people what they need to learn in order to be successful. More importantly, as leaders they create in people the desire to use their skills to achieve great things.

The Motivating Positive Influence Leader

For some people, their pivotal influence came in the workplace when they encountered a manager who "saw something in me" or "pushed me to do something different" or "held me accountable." The motivating manager often identifies some untapped part of you that was previously unknown to you as, for example, in the "Blind Spot" of the *Johari Window* (J. Luft & H. Ingham, 1995).

Facebook COO Sheryl Sandberg, author of the best-seller, *Lean In* (2013), says Harvard's Larry Summers was a major motivational figure in her life and a lifelong advocate for women. Sandberg worked for Summers at both the World Bank and the U.S. Treasury Department and learned much from him. At the World Bank he encouraged ministers from other countries to invest in the education of women in finance and economics. At Treasury, he fought for social security benefits for women working in their homes, better enforcement of child support obligations, and an expansion of childcare tax credits.

Steve Jobs served as a mentor and advisor to Mark Zuckerberg. The two often met to discuss management practices. Zuckerberg credits Jobs with helping him understand that "what you build can change the world."

Roxanne, a nurse manager in a hospital-based cancer center who we interviewed, said the motivating leader in her work life was Dr. Dan Fram, a radiation oncologist. It was his caring approach to patients and the key moments they spent together that convinced her that "oncology provides me with the best opportunity to help people."

Jim, a candidate for Congress we interviewed, learned from his priest, when he was studying to become a priest himself, that a "spiritual influence" must have solid life experience—been there, done that. They must be committed to your success, able to teach you the things that really matter, including how to prepare yourself for life and, most important, they must be spiritually aligned with you.

The Successful Motivating Positive Influence Leader

Effective leaders are motivators who see things in people they often do not see in themselves. They help people realize their potential by showing them the way... while not doing it for them.

The Role Model Positive Influence Leader

"The greatest thing about Michael Jordan was that he was never afraid to fail," said LeBron James of his boyhood idol back in 2013. Every fan of basketball during those days will recall that Jordan never feared failure, which is why he was always called upon to take the biggest shots in the biggest games. He viewed failure as part of his success and a key ingredient to his learning and development. After 10 years as a professional player, two championships, and multiple league MVPs, LeBron James confessed that one of his biggest obstacles was fear of failure. He said, "I want to succeed so bad that I became afraid of failing." LeBron still wants to be the greatest player of all time, but fear of failure is something he has yet to master, something his role model, Michael Jordan, did.

Kobe Bryant, another of the great basketball players of all time said, "The impact that Jordan had on me, from when I was just a kid, is immeasurable. I wanted to be just as good as him and I wanted to have the same kind of impact on the game."

And now, both LeBron James and Kobe Bryant have become role models to the next generation of players. Paul George, a current NBA All-Star, grew up in Los Angeles watching Kobe Bryant play. George says:

> I mean, part of the reason I'm here is because of him. He sent me to the gym when I was a kid to work on my game. I tried to be like him. I watched him and tried to copy him.

From our study group, Adriana shared a story about Dina Habib Powell, former deputy to National Security Council for Strategy under President Donald Trump. Adriana and Dina attended the same prep school for girls, Ursuline Academy of Dallas, where she first met Dina and heard her speak to the students of her school. Dina is a former senior non-profit financial executive with Goldman Sachs, a philanthropist, and a U.S. policymaker (she is the former assistant secretary of state for educational and cultural affairs in the George W. Bush administration) before her most recent role with the Obama administration. In addition, Dina was born in Cairo, Egypt. When she came with her family to the United States at the age of 4, she could not speak any English.

Part of Dina's responsibility as the deputy to the National Security Council for Strategy was preparing for dignitaries when they visit the White House. Dina shared with the group, "Deep policy thinking matters and so does setting the dinner table properly." Dina spoke about how getting things done right includes paying close attention to the details that really matter. Adriana told us:

> Dina wanted to make an impact on the world and as an immigrant woman she could relate to who wanted to serve and make an impact. I could see in Dina that it was possible to be an immigrant woman of global impact.

Danny, one of the consultants from our research group, spoke of his mother as a role model, and he often thinks of her in his work when trying to best understand his client's situation. "My mother was the most empathetic person I have ever known. She opened my eyes up to walking in another person's shoes to understand them and what is driving them and that there is always more to the story." Danny shared that his missteps and failures in life have in large part come as a result of a failure to be empathetic.

Marlon Brando is among the greatest actors of all time and has influenced many of the great actors of today, some of whom he influenced without having met them. Dustin Hoffman, an Oscar winner, shared that his acting was inspired by Marlon Brando. He referred to Brando as "the be-all and end-all." Russell Crowe once recorded a song titled "I Want to Be like Marlon Brando." James Dean, Paul Newman, and Robert De Niro adapted Brando's method acting approach, and several others mimicked his relentless preparation for roles.

Brando indirectly influenced a generation of actors by shifting their approach away from the British classically stage-trained style to Brando's method acting. An entire generation of actors influenced by one actor, most of whom they never met. Jack Nicholson said, "This man has been my idol all of my professional life, and I don't think I'm alone in that." As a young man growing up in New Jersey, Jack had a summer job working as an assistant manager of a movie theater. It was there that he watched Brando in *On the Waterfront* countless times. "Even before I thought about acting (or met Brando), he influenced me strongly."

Politicians have role models, too. Many Republican politicians say they revere former President Ronald Reagan as a paragon of conservatism. Dr. Ben Carson, secretary of Housing and Urban Development in the Trump administration, credits Reagan for converting him to the Republican Party just as Reagan did in 1951. In the 2015 Republican primaries, Reagan's name was mentioned 64 times in the September candidate debate. Incidentally, on the Democratic side, no former president's name has been mentioned even a fraction of that time.

It has been close to 30 years since Reagan left office, and the party is still searching for his heir apparent. Many in the party saw his presidency as a golden age during which they defeated communism and restored America as a "shining city on a hill." In addition, many experts inside the party believe that the two Bush family presidencies lacked the success of the Reagan presidency because they failed to follow the Reagan ideological blueprint even though George W. Bush often compared himself to Reagan.

Ironically, Reagan is unlike any of the Republican politicians who have compared themselves to him. Reagan compromised on several agreements with the Democrats, showing a pragmatic side that would be considered blasphemous by today's standards; e.g., large tax increases and amnesty for undocumented immigrants. He was content getting 80 percent of what he hoped to achieve if it meant he had to give on 20 percent. Reagan navigated the issues of complexity with his plain-spoken style and his simple truths. As a result, his legacy is intact as a role model positive influence leader for many in the Republican Party.

Role Models as Positive Influence Leaders

When great leaders serve as positive influence role models, they must always ensure their actions match their words, provide clear examples of how things are done properly, and push people beyond their assumed limits.

Looking Back: Some Issues to Consider

It's clear that behind all of us, or maybe standing next to us, is a person who was that game-changer "without whom I would not be the person I am today." They are that special positive influence who supported you, taught you, motivated you, or served as a role model for you on your journey.

We want to help you be that special kind of leader by identifying and cataloguing the essential characteristics of the four types or styles of positive influence leader. We provide a blueprint to help you become an effective and successful positive influence leader using any one or more of the four styles. We will also layout a framework for those who wish to achieve that transformational level of positive influence leader.

In the pages that follow, we will share what we learned from the approximately 50 people we interviewed. Our study group represents a diverse group of people that include men, women, young, old, white, African American, Hispanic, Asian-American, and foreign-born doing a wide variety of jobs in multiple industries. They include a CEO, many senior corporate managers, several physicians, a nurse, a fitness instructor, a museum curator, a psychiatrist, a martial arts guru, a learning consultant, a lead singer in a rock band, a schoolteacher, a marathon runner, and many others.

Positive Influence

1. Looking back, who were the positive influences in your life? In what ways did they influence you?
2. What current or past famous person has had a positive influence on your life?
3. In what ways is it possible to be influenced by someone without ever having met them?
4. Is there someone you would describe as your role model? Describe the person.

Part 2

The Four Types of Positive Influence Leaders

Chapter 3
The Supportive Leader

> *We know the impressionist painter Vincent Van Gogh from his famous paintings such as Starry Night, Self-Portrait and Vase with Red Poppies. However, we may never have known about Van Gogh were it not for the support of his friend, Paul Gauguin, who encouraged Van Gogh to paint from memory using his imagination rather than trying to create a literal picture.**

The supportive leader believes in people and encourages them to believe in themselves. You can hear her say, "You got this," or "You can do it," or "I'm here for you." However, effective support is more than catchy phrases ("All for one, one for all") or tired clichés ("Be the change you want to see"). It must be sincere and believable. People we interviewed told us that when their mother or their boss said, "I'm with you all the way," it was pretty easy to know if it came from the heart.

When a leader is supportive, they:

- believe that you have what it takes to be successful whatever the goal may be.
- make it clear that they are backing you.
- instill a belief that anything you are facing is achievable.
- coach the person to the point where they believe they can handle things that come their way.
- provide specific help to a person that goes beyond encouragement and is necessary for the accomplishment of their goals and the realization of their dreams.
- help people see the many possibilities available to them and help them choose the best path forward.
- believe in you even when you do you not believe in yourself.
- bolster the team's sense that they can come up with a viable solution.

*Deborah Mancoff, *"Vincent Van Gogh's Biography"*

- encourage members of their team to be understanding of and helpful to each other.
- insist that people on their team do things the right way.

Many people in the course of their life benefit from being around a supportive positive influence leader. Our research indicates that especially early in your life this is often a parent; later you may encounter a supportive teacher, coach, or mentor and, if you are fortunate, a workplace manager as that positive influence leader who supports your growth as a professional. We will look at the many ways supportive leaders are a positive influence on the people in their life.

Supportive Parents

For many people, the first person to support them was a parent or a grandparent. A mother or father is there at a very young age to lift you up, make it clear they have your back, help you overcome your fears, develop your self-esteem, and encourage an independent self-reliance.

The supportive leader often believes in you even when you may not believe in yourself. More specifically, they see something in you that you have yet to see in yourself. It's there, but you have not yet become aware of it and, more importantly, aware of your ability to be good at it. Actress, dancer, and author Victoria Rowell credits her foster mother with seeing "something" in her, giving her ballet lessons when she was eight years old, and encouraging her passion for the arts while giving her the courage to pursue her dreams. Rowell's dreams became a reality as she joined the American Ballet Theater and the Juilliard School of Music and Dance.

For almost 20 years, she appeared as Drucilla in the daytime TV series *The Young and the Restless,* where she was nominated three times for a Daytime Emmy Award and received multiple NAACP Image Awards (Wikipedia contributors, 2019, June 27).

In a related example, Shirnette, born and brought up in Jamaica, West Indies, talked of her grandmother who raised her, taught her to read and write, and gave her "pure love." However, it was also "tough love" that included high expectations for studying, reading, and getting high grades. For example, in the fourth grade, she got spanked because she only got a seventy on a test. The support of her grandmother also included learning life skills such as farming and sewing. In addition to practical skills, she took from her grandmother a caring and desire to help and care for others. When her grandmother developed cancer, Shirnette decided to become an oncologist and, as she said, "become an advocate for others who cannot be an advocate for themselves."

Supportive leaders are able to achieve a delicate balance between empowering members of their team while staying involved with them. The message is: You are free to figure out the best way to get it done, to use resources, involve others, and make decisions, but I am still here for you.

In an entirely different field, but in a similar manner, Jennifer, a senior curator at the Smithsonian's National Museum of American History, says her mother

> instilled in her a passion for history at a very early age. Their home was full of history. In fact, her mother restored their Federal-style home to what it was like in 1810 down to the type of type of paint, siding, colors, and furnishings. Her mother's love of history, especially American history, inspired Jennifer to pursue a college degree in American history.

Jennifer's mother was a supportive leader who encouraged, nudged, pushed, or simply placed her in a situation that got her to believe in herself and do things she may have only dreamed of doing. Jennifer said her mother told her many times, "Don't let anyone stop you from doing something you've never done before." Later, when Jennifer got her first job as a curator at the Smithsonian, her mother said, "You have my dream job."

"My mother was the most empathic person I have ever known," Danny, an executive recruiter, told us. He learned so much from her because she always thought about the other person's life and their personal story. Early on, he said, "It opened my eyes to the idea of walking in another person's shoes in order to understand what is driving them." On his desk sits the phrase "There's always more to the story." Danny shared this personal insight with us. "My mistakes and failures have come as a result of not being sufficiently empathic."

A parent is often the very first positive influence in your life as they instill, often at a young age, a love of something and belief that you can be successful in doing that something. For example, world-famous, award-winning actor Denzel Washington was a big influence on his son, John

David Washington. John, who initially did not want to be in his father's shadow, began his work life as a professional football player. However, things changed when HBO's casting director, Sheila Jaffe, was having trouble casting someone who looked like a real football player for the series *Ballers*. She reached out to Denzel's agent to inquire about the availability of John David and, as they say, the rest is history. *Ballers* is now in its fourth season and going strong. Along the way, John David picked up the lead role in Spike Lee's very successful *Black Klansman*. While son John David admires his father as an actor, he says:

> *"If I try to act like him or make movie choices like him, I'm going to fail. I love him. He's one of my favorite actors of all time but I can't do that. Nobody can do that." However, Denzel is a positive influence because what he did was, in his son's words, "pass on the lesson and legacy of hard work, how to be an African American man in this country and how to honor the craft and work hard."* (Igoe, 2019).

By their very role, parents have the first opportunity to be a supportive positive influence. Parents are leaders in the lives of their children as they, by actions big and small, send a message that you have what it takes to be successful. The very same skills that make for a supportive parent contribute to your success as a positive influence leader in the workplace.

Supportive Teachers, Coaches, and Mentors

Effective leaders support in a way that works for the person. They don't push them out there on their own without preparing them. Sometimes they even have to clear the path forward. Support is always situational because as a leader you may find that the person needs you to shield them from an obstacle whether that obstacle is a difficult person or a challenging task.

American actress Viola Davis has talked often about how supportive Meryl Streep has been to her since they appeared together in the Broadway production of *Doubt*. In fact, before Davis went onstage to accept her 2017 Oscar for Best Supporting Actress in *Fences*, she stopped to give Streep a kiss and a hug. They often exchange phone calls and notes. Davis has said Streep says things that make her feel that "what I have is enough." In other words, being supportive in this case means "You are good enough to be successful, you don't need to feel lesser than."

With all her awards and other forms of recognition Streep is an entertainment industry leader, especially among women, and she takes that responsibility seriously. As her relationship with Davis makes clear, a few words of support from Streep can be a game changer. Davis is building her own collection of awards. She is the only African American actress to win a Tony, Oscar, and an Emmy (Ma, 2017).

During the early years of his corporate career, Tony said his mentor often "stepped in front of me because I worked for a difficult boss." However, his mentor knew that support of this type should not be a long-term strategy but a way of learning "how to navigate things at work."

Teachers are leaders who teach you things you need to learn, but they can also be supportive leaders who foster a "can-do" mentality. They believe in your ability to learn, grow, develop, and do things you never thought possible. They encourage you to "try it" while being right there to show you the way or catch you if you fall.

Betsy, a woman we interviewed, was studying theater in college assuming her true north was acting, writing, and directing. However, the course of study included a required course in technical theater where the focus was on lighting, sound, and set design. During the course, Jim, the instructor, assigned Betsy to go up on a tall ladder and hang lights on a clamp high above the stage. As Betsy recounts the situation now with a typical sense of humor, she says, "I had never been on a ladder. I was a little Jewish girl. We never even had a ladder in our house. But Jim said, 'Betsy, you can do it,' and I believed him."

This was a game changer for Betsy. As she told us, "In those days, no one would send a woman to do something technical in the theater. From there I began using power tools, learned how to build a set, and wire everything on a stage."

Supreme Court Justice Sonia Sotomayor said attorney Jose' Cabranes supported her by making it clear that she could be a great attorney while still maintaining and taking great pride in her Puerto Rican heritage. In turn, Justice Sotomayor is an inspiration to many Hispanic women who aspire to achieve great things, too (Ma, 2017).

Bob, an African American management consultant in our study group, recalled fondly time spent as a 12-year old hanging around the local barber shop in his neighborhood in Elizabeth, New Jersey.

The barber, Mr. Sampson, introduced Bob and other young men to black history in a town where the public-school curriculum did not include anything about the history of famous black Americans. These experiences of looking at the pictures on the wall of the barber shop and talking with Mr. Sampson and the other people in the shop helped Bob learn and understand his heritage and, as he said, "think of myself in a positive light.

Sometimes being a supportive leader requires that you give the person confidence that they can achieve their goals. Peter, a medical oncologist, spoke of Dr. Zwicker, his mentor in college who gave him an opportunity to work in his lab as an undergraduate. His willingness to let Peter work in the lab gave him confidence as did having him work on his projects.

Ultimately, he made Peter co-author of an article based on their work in the lab. Dr. Zwicker saw that Peter lacked confidence because he came to the United States from Korea with limited knowledge of the English language and culture. However, as Peter said, "He let me come along when he saw patients which, in turn, inspired me to go to medical school." From these experiences with Dr. Zwicker, I learned that "You create your own barriers and you need to break down those barriers because no one can do it for you."

Sometimes you can be influenced by a mentor you've never met. You are influenced in a positive way by learning about their life story, being inspired by it, and incorporating their life lessons. Oprah Winfrey first learned about Maya Angelou when she read *I Know Why the Caged Bird Sings*. Oprah immediately felt connected to her because her life mirrored Angelou's upbringing in the South. She found support because it validated her experience (I'm OK). Years later, the two met and the bond was instant. As Oprah says, "She's the woman who can share my triumphs, chide me with hard truth, and soothe me with words of comfort when I call her in my deepest pain."

As Oprah Winfrey's relationship with Maya Angelou makes abundantly clear, the supportive leader will be there for you, but also tell you the "hard truth," provide needed guidance, and help you get to the next level (Fradkin, 2017).

Teachers help you learn critical skills, but they also support your need for continuous learning and often give you support and encouragement to take on life's challenges. A coach, whether a football coach or a life coach, is often that person who knows your strengths and insecurities and is able to support your growth and development. An effective mentor can show you the way to success while helping you overcome barriers (including those of your own creation) that stand in the way of achieving your life goals. If your goal is to be a supportive positive influence workplace leader, at times you must be an effective mentor, coach, or teacher.

Supportive Spouses and Significant Others

No one makes it out here alone. We all need people along the way who support our workplace goals as we, over time, pursue our career. Work-life balance is a catch phrase that is often overworked and underachieved. Just as we value teamwork in business, it is just as important in our personal life. Couples, especially, need to support each other at home in a way that contributes to workplace success. Our research clearly indicates that supportive spouses have very positive influences on career success.

For example, one of the most supportive people in Roxanne's life is her husband. Roxanne, an oncology nurse in a regional, hospital-based cancer center, found her true north because her husband convinced her to make a significant career change. However, it was not easy because the career change required returning to school, specifically nursing school, and completing a challenging curriculum while working full-time. She did it, however, with the positive support of her husband who saw something in her, believed she could do more, and convinced her that she could be something more. Roxanne told us:

> He didn't just talk. He took over certain family responsibilities that allowed Roxanne to more easily deal with the twin demands of work and study. As he said to her, "This is our life now, time to start a new chapter." Once she recognized that happiness comes from within, she was able to do something that made her feel good and that translates to her patients who see her as accessible, kind, and caring.

This is another example of a leader who is not only encouraging and supportive but clears the path for the person making it possible for them to succeed.

In a similar vein, Judy had a dream of opening a retail business but lacked both experience and confidence. She had worked for years as a preschool teacher, but always kept that dream alive as she studied comparable businesses, made notes, checked out possible sites, and talked to other retailers. At one point she talked with her husband who quickly said, "I'm in. Let's do it." He was able to arrange his work schedule so that he could help her find a suitable location, create a business plan, meet with suppliers, and find ways to finance the operation. He believed in and supported Judy, but something more was needed—a partner who, while she takes the lead, does some of the necessary behind-the-scenes work to move the project forward and be there once it takes off.

Nancy, a senior manager in the insurance industry, is another woman with a very supportive husband.

> He stayed home with the kids so I could build my career. This was especially important because I did a good bit of business travel, and he handled the kids without a complaint. He also pushed me to do things I might not have done. During this time I had a very demanding boss, but my husband encouraged me to hang in there—"you can do it," he said.

Mindi, who works with an outreach program for survivors of sexual violence, said her husband, Adam, was the first and most important positive influence on her life. "I was a victim of sexual abuse and a drug user when I met him. He was the first person to say he liked me and why—for my gifts and for my potential. He said I needed help and offered to help me and to be there for me. His unconditional support helped me get clean. I realized my worth and that I wanted to this for someone else." Mindi is now a positive influence leader for other abused women through her resource center in south Florida.

The notion of a spouse or significant other being that person in your life that is a supportive positive influence is understandable. The same positive influence skills of encouragement, strong belief, and tangible actions are critical to your success as a supportive, positive influence leader in the workplace.

Supportive Managers

At times, all you need is a manager to say, "I'm here for you, if you need me, but you can do it yourself. I know it." However, at other times and with other people, being a supportive leader requires that you take it to the next level by either paving the way or setting the conditions that make it possible for you to succeed or empowering you to take action on you own. One specific situation that we have encountered involves giving the person a specific task or position that you are confident they have the experience or skills to handle and then encouraging and empowering them to act.

For Esther it was a move from a position as director of small Hispanic Arts Program at Rutgers University to head up a major Special Projects unit of the National Endowment for the Arts (NEA). In this case, the supportive leader was Mary Ann at NEA who knew that Esther's skills were a perfect match for the new position. Esther told us during her interview, "She got me to believe in myself."

Similarly, politician, businessperson, and former presidential candidate Mitt Romney says that William Bain, founder of Bain Capital, saw something in him and, as Romney said, "gave me the opportunity of a lifetime when hired me at Bain. He put me in a position to succeed and I did."

Jody, a senior manager at a major medical device, pharmaceutical, and consumer products company, had no trouble naming her first boss, Cliff, as a very supportive positive influence in her career. Cliff was a great manager, Jodi said, "whose high energy and out-of-box thinking was infectious to the point that it helped build my confidence." As a result, Jody said, "He got me to do things I would not have dreamed I could do."

Along the way "He connected me to other people in the company while positioning me in places that I would not have felt comfortable going on my own." Although he did not hold the title of mentor, Cliff was one of those people who is able, by his actions, to instill a belief in a person that "anything is achievable."

Fresh out of Harvard Business School, Mark went to work for AT&T where he encountered his first boss, Richard, who greeted him on his first day with a long "welcome aboard" note. "Richard talked about the opportunities ahead of me. He was a very supportive manager who always included me in important meetings, treated me with great respect, listened actively to what I said, and helped further my career." Mark told us that Richard was very smart and, yet despite his elevated status in the company, remained always humble.

Many of the people we interviewed were fortunate to work for a supportive positive influence manager early in their career. Their manager was a positive influence because he or she quickly made them feel part of the team; they belonged; they could do the job and do it well, and they gave them the confidence to take on new challenges on their own.

Looking Back: Some Issues to Consider

A supportive positive influence leader fosters a belief that "you can do it" while making it clear they are backing you. They coach you, perhaps mentor you and often help you see that you already have all you need to be successful. A supportive leader also applies the same approach to her team. She clearly indicates to the team that they have all the skills and resources to be successful and, with that foundation, she empowers them to get the job or complete the project with minimal oversight.

The effective positive influence leader knows exactly when a member of their team needs a supportive leadership style, one that involves encouragement, reassurance, praise, or perhaps, just a simple "I'm here for you at all times."

1. Who have been the supportive positive influences in your life? What did they do that was critical to your success?
2. What is the central message of the vignette about the relationship between Viola Davis and Meryl Streep? What is the key learning there that you can take back and apply in your role as a positive influence leader in the workplace?
3. What do you think of the statement by Peter "You create your own barriers and you need to break down those barriers because no one can do it for you"?
4. What are some of the specific takeaways from this chapter that you can apply in your daily work life to become a more effective supportive positive influence leader?

Chapter 4
The Teacher Leader

> *Jane Fonda made the movie "On Golden Pond" for her father, but it was Katherine Hepburn who taught Fonda important life lessons. Fonda has said that Hepburn taught her to be self-conscious, to have a presence, to have a style that is uniquely yours. From Hepburn she learned to pay attention to herself and that style is important.**

The teacher leader is sometimes a schoolteacher or college professor but often is someone who just happens to be able to teach you the things you need to learn. Our experience tells us that the great teacher leaders do something more than teach. They create in you the desire to learn, to develop the skills and knowledge to be your best self. We have all known subject matter experts who were smart, very smart, and able to do the job better than just about anyone. However, they were unable to inspire others to learn and lacked the capacity to impart to others their knowledge or train them to acquire the necessary skills.

The teacher leader is able to:

- inspire people to want to learn.
- teach people in a way that is suited to their learning style.
- create a desire to be the best in life and work.
- train people in the necessary problem-solving skills rather than solve the problem for them.
- thoughtfully instruct people in the challenges of the real world.
- insist that people do things the right way.
- identify those teachable moments when someone is open to learning.
- help people believe that failure can be a necessary step in the journey to success.
- create an atmosphere where people respect the strengths of their teammates.
- get people to acknowledge the skills and knowledge they already possess.

*Julia Ma, "25 Famous Women on Their Role Models," *The Cut,* Jan. 26, 2017

Positive Influence Teachers: Teaching What You Need to Learn

As we said, sometimes the teacher leader is actually someone who holds the position of teacher, professor, or coach. For example, Leslie, a woman we interviewed, told us about Professor Carlson who was first and foremost so passionate about teaching that he inspired Leslie to be a great teacher. In addition to teaching many practical teaching skills, she said, "It was his energy and charisma that made me want to be not just a teacher, but to be a great teacher."

We also interviewed Rob, the young lead singer with an indie rock band who credits several teachers with instilling in him the importance of creativity. His high school creative writing and art teachers both went beyond talking about the importance of creativity to pushing him to let those creative thoughts drive his passion. As a young person these teacher leaders challenged him to try different types of thinking modes and be willing to challenge conventional ideas about music. Their influence informs his artistic side, and he believes it has made him a better and more successful songwriter.

A teacher and clinical psychologist in a Ph.D. nursing program helped Gina develop an alternative set of values than the one she brought to the program. As Gina put it, "I learned from Debbie that we don't need to reject our parents' values, but we can move on to incorporate a new set of values. For example, I learned that people get better when we connect with them or as she put it, 'we are only as healthy as the relationships we're in.'"

In our interview with Tony, he had great praise for his martial arts instructor, Gary, who pushed him hard by creating a challenging environment. He believed "Excellence is the only way." So, as a teacher leader, Gary always pushed each student just beyond their personal limits. Tony learned that the goal of becoming a martial arts expert through personal trial was challenging yet worth achieving. He passes that message along in his martial arts classes today.

For some people a teacher early in their life can be a real game changer. For Anne, a senior financial services executive, it was a ninth-grade math teacher who "saw something in me. He saw that I knew the answers in class, but not on the test." Rather than just let me fail, he called my home, and in the course of the conversation said, "Anne is an A student who is doing D work right now." Her father did not get mad. Anne said, "He just gave me that look." And that was enough. Anne had been obsessed with a boy in the class and didn't want him to think she was a math geek. However, after the call by the teacher, she said to herself, "He (her crush) would have to put up with her being an A student and not cool."

Hedge fund manager Mark was fortunate to work with Paul, a very successful investor and hedge fund manager. As Mark told us, "After the '87 crash, Paul called a bull market and I did not. I screwed up." However, Paul taught him the importance of moving on and never letting your ego get in the way of decision-making. Paul told him:

> When you make mistakes, you have to forgive yourself; not agonize over them but learn from them. If you did your best, that was enough to move on and figure it out for your next opportunity.

Teacher positive influence leaders are often mentors as in the case of Jim, a business owner, a priest, and former candidate for Congress. Jim describes Paul, a faculty member at St. John's University:

> He introduced me to social justice and liberation theology. He shaped my belief system. For example, when I was a soccer coach, we refused to wear Nike products because of their treatment of employees at their overseas factories. And he and I volunteered together in a program for recovering addicts.
>
> Jim thought I was a pain in the ass as a student, but when I was ready to be a serious student, he as a teacher would appear. He also taught me to follow my passions, my heart, and whatever gets me up in the morning. He shared Gandhi's belief that when work is for a just cause, people will pop out of the pavement.

Positive Influence Coaches: Uncovering Your Untapped Strengths

Pro football great and Super Bowl champion Darrell Green talks about how he was mentored by his middle school football coach who taught him what it takes to be a great running athlete. He helped Green identify possibilities, things he never envisioned as possibilities, but were possible if he learned, worked hard, and was persistent (Rhodes, Sept. 13, 2016).

Brad Gilbert, who many consider one of the best tennis coaches of all time, taught multiple grand slam champion, Andre Agassi that "...coaches aren't measured by what they know, but by *what their students learn*. Agassi said Gilbert "...taught me that in tennis you don't have to be perfect. You don't even have to be good. You have to be better than one person. That's what's called problem-solving. That's what you call simple."

One day after a practice session that did not go well, Brad told Andre that "Tomorrow will be better." When Agassi asked how he knew it would be better, Gilbert said, "I'm a stats guy. I look at the odds and I know there is no way you can play any [worse] than you played today" (*Inside Tennis*, May 13, 2019).

A pharmaceutical company senior manager, Debra, told us that Kate, an organizational consultant, taught her to be more self-aware. Debra told us, "Kate helped me identify my shortcomings and yet feel good about myself by pointing out my positive attributes as well as my successes."

Mentors are often teacher leaders because they have more experience, they have been where you want to go, and have made the mistakes from which you can learn. As Sheila Worthington of Catalyst—an organization that works to advance women in business—says, "Having a good mentor may be more important than hard work and talent." Mentors can teach what you need to learn to operate effectively in the world of work (Nelson, June 25, 2017).

Another person we interviewed, Betsy, learned from her significant other. Rich taught her how to break down a job into specific tasks and then how to give instructions to people in a way that they can understand and use. She has carried these principles with her in all her management positions.

To be an effective search consultant in financial services you need a mentor or coach to teach you how to be effective in such a unique industry. Danny was fortunate to work for Susan during his college years. She taught him how to be a successful professional. Susan taught him how to be "fearless" and deal with failure. The key thing he learned from her was that "the focus has to be on the needs of the broker, not the firm where he is employed." Throughout their time together, she fired him up, was generous in sharing her expertise, but "...she always held me accountable."

In a similar vein, Sonia had a most profound impact on Stuart in the area of personal growth. Prior to working with her:

> I avoided showing emotions; tried to avoid or evade people, but she put me on a path to self-awareness such that I learned how I am and what I own. I became a true advisor and not just a consultant. Sonia taught me to worry about myself and that my work could help other people. I learned the importance of "Take care of yourself so you can take care of others." I learned from her learning how to fail because you will never learn your potential or your limits until you put yourself where you could fail.

All healthcare professionals who work with oncology patients need to learn how to deal with the possibilities that many of their patients will die. Oncology nurse Roxanne told us she learned much about death from her mentor, Dr. Fram, a radiation oncologist who said, "Death is a part of life and it's our job to help people accept and deal with their situation." Most important, "Patients are not defined by their cancer." One of the biggest learnings for Roxanne was that it is important to learn about the patients, including who they are, and what drives them. From Dr. Fram she also learned that she had to accept that, despite our best efforts, some might die.

Positive Influence Managers: Facilitating Your Learning and Development

Famed film and television producer and entertainment executive Ely Landau was the prototypical teacher leader. Landau started his career producing and directing for television and later for the movies. Among his many accomplishments was "King," a documentary about the public life of Dr. Martin Luther King. He was generous in sharing his experience and advising people who wanted to be part of the production side of the entertainment business. One such person was Larry, a member of our study group. Larry was a division leader in a summer camp attended by Landau's two boys. At the end of the summer he thanked Larry for doing a good job with his boys and said if he ever needed a job, all he had to do was call.

Sometime later, Larry called Landau and asked if that job offer was serious. Landau asked, "Where are you?" to which Larry responded, "Philadelphia." Landau said, "It's eleven thirty. If you're not here by three-thirty, you're late for work."

Landau sensed Larry's enthusiasm, his knack for quickly picking up concepts, and his willingness to work hard. As a result, he was willing to teach him the business. Here we have an excellent example of the leader who teaches a person the things they need to learn to be successful. And Larry was extremely successful going from National Television Associates to CBS-TV to RKO, later to Viacom and finally, MGM where he worked for Kirk Kerkorian. This story also demonstrates the importance of the person being a ready and willing learner or in the words of that overused quote "When the student is ready, the teacher will appear."

One of the big takeaways for Larry was something Landau said to him early on in his career that became a significant life lesson:

> You will be selling yourself a lot longer than you will be selling for my company. **Don't ever do anything that you are uncomfortable with**.

Warren Buffett, CEO of Berkshire Hathaway and legendary investor, and Bill Gates, founder of Microsoft, have built a famous relationship over the years. Gates says that Buffett taught him how to manage his time better by prioritizing certain people and tasks. He also gave Gates his favorite business book, *Business Journeys* by John Brooks. It is now Gates' favorite business book. And, of course, they have teamed up on many philanthropic causes and *The Giving Pledge* where billionaires pledge to give away half of their fortune.

One of the most famous teacher-pupil relationships in the art world is that of the legendary French impressionist Pierre-August Renoir and the much younger Pierre Bonnard. They met at the funeral of another artist and quickly became friends and colleagues often visiting one another's homes and studios. Bonnard admired Renoir's paintings of half-dressed and nude figures.

Renoir was a mentor to Bonnard such that during one of their frequent walks Renoir said, "Bonnard, you have to embellish." Renoir's seemingly simple recommendation was life-altering because Bonnard almost immediately applied that advice to his painting *Reclining Nude*, by adding a brightly colored fabric to the foreground and a vivid landscape in the background.

Gerald, a participant in our study, had a long career with GE as an engineer. During the early years he started out in materials management where his first manager was a classic teacher leader. She taught Gerald how to manage large projects and, more importantly, how to engage plant leadership in such a way that they will accept the necessary changes that are an inevitable aspect of such projects. And perhaps even more essential, she taught him how to manage himself in ways that will enhance his career opportunities. One critical piece of advice: "If you are not sure, don't fake and stumble through it. Just say so, own up to it, figure it out, or get help and put it right."

Jody, a senior-level manager in the pharmaceutical industry, told us her first boss was a significant positive influence from whom she learned the importance of an uncluttered mind. She said:

> He helped me think through things and prioritize issues. He also heightened my awareness of the importance of the corporate credo and culture as the foundation for making solid decisions. The result of his role as a teacher leader is that...I was empowered to go to people in business operations and say, "Let's rethink how we are doing this and how it is impacted by the credo and the culture."

Similarly, Jennifer, our museum curator, learned from a senior curator how to "get stuff done in the organization" and the importance of having "a strong work ethic." Perhaps most important, he taught me that "You have to be able to do things in order to manage people who are doing those things."

Gissoo, a patient advocacy manager with a pharmaceutical company, said the head of the oncology business unit helped her learn so much about the organization. She would say, "Gissoo, go interview these 10 people this week—find out what they do; what makes them tick." She was, by this learning methodology, helping me learn what I needed to know about how the company worked and what each unit and each person did. By this process I broadened my business knowledge, which, in turn gave me a long-term view of the organization. The net result was that I became be a more effective patient advocate.

Highly regarded sportswriter Nancy benefited greatly from her editor Terry Taylor at the Associated Press. Nancy told us:

> I learned from Terry the importance of attention to detail because she was an incredible editor who missed nothing. I learned the simple truth of the value of hard work. For example, one time while Terry was in China, I got a call from at what was 5 a.m. local time wanting to talk about something I had written. And finally, I learned the importance of determination. As Terry said, "Don't be concerned with what others think. Keep your eyes forward and just keep doing your job."

Dave, a former CEO of a major financial services company, learned from his boss, that "the right way" involved teamwork and working together with his colleagues rather than competing with them. At first, Dave viewed a colleague as a competitor, even a threat, but his boss encouraged him to get know the person, to understand what makes him tick, and, most important, his virtues and value to the company. As a result, Dave eventually saw the person as a valued colleague rather than a competitor.

Positive Influence Parents: Sharing Important Work-Life Values

Eliza Steele, chief executive of Jive Software, says her father was a huge positive influence teaching her the importance of focusing on what's important and prioritizing the tasks in front of you. This was an important learning for anyone in business faced with making key decisions because it's imperative that you make decisions in the context of the most important things. It's all part of staying focused on the company vision (Bryant, May 28, 2017).

Both a supportive and teacher positive influence, Debra's mother shared this simple but profound guiding philosophy. "You can be anything you want to be, but it's a whole lot easier if you're good at it."

Ramon, another interviewee, grew up on a farm in rural Spain. From his grandfather, he learned the importance of getting up early, working hard, and in general developing a great work ethic. He has carried this work ethic with him all his life as he still gets up early, never stops because he's tired, and, if necessary, works overtime to get the job done. In addition, his grandfather taught him the value of always having a high energy level and a positive attitude.

Frank, a psychiatrist in our study group, learned much from his physician father. However, the learnings were not medical or technical, but rather a set of values concerning how to treat patients and others you meet in the course of your life. Frank learned the importance of treating everyone with dignity and courtesy—to be respectful of others and to listen in a nonjudgmental way. His father said, "All patient stories are sacred. We are all part of the human family. Do not treat people as 'other.'"

Beth, an instructional designer we interviewed, said her father "taught me technical stuff, like how to program, which, in turn, sparked my interest in computers." However, most important, Beth said she learned by watching him work when, as a high school student, she worked in the same organization. As many people told us, from the great teacher leaders you learn more than skills and knowledge; you learn how to work, to prioritize, to make decisions, to listen, to work with others on a team, and to take responsibility for your actions.

Looking Back: Some Issues to Consider

The teacher leader can be an inspiring figure in your life in a specific way. He motivates you to learn, to advance your knowledge, to develop your skill set, and be more proficient in your daily work life. He often helps you recognize and use the talents you already possess but have not acknowledged or been reluctant to use. The learning may include positive values and an ethical mindset that provide the underpinning for an insistence on doing things "the right way."

The positive influence teacher leader is careful to teach the necessary problem-solving skills but not solve the problem for the person. Similarly, a mistake or an error must be acknowledged and seen as an opportunity to develop resilience and learn new habits. The learning may also include making the person aware of the harsh realities of the world and how to negotiate them.

1. Some teacher positive influence leaders challenge you to try different things, to be more effective. Who, in the course of your life, has challenged you to try different things, to be more effective?

2. What do you think of the advice by Debra's mother: "You can be anything you want to be, but it's a lot easier if you're good at it?"
3. In your experience, what has been most important for you to learn from that positive influence person in your life: a values system or a set of skills and knowledge?
4. Thinking back to a time when things did not go well for you, to what extent were you able to adopt the advice that Paul gave to Mark: "When you make mistakes, you have to forgive yourself, not to agonize over them, but to learn from them." If you did your best, is it enough to move on and figure it out for your next opportunity?"

Chapter 5
The Motivating Leader

> *Actress, singer, and dancer Chita Rivera credits her dance teacher, Doris Jones, as the motivating force in her life. Jones loved to dance as a child but being black, she was not admitted to any ballet schools. She learned to dance on her own and later opened one of the nation's first ballet schools for children of color. Jones taught Rivera to dance but most importantly to "work hard because you don't get anything free... you really have to work for it." When George Ballanchine's School of American Ballet asked Rivera to audition, she was nervous because all the girls were very tall and thin and she said to Jones, "Oh, I'm short and Puerto Rican." Jones replied, "Now, Conchita, you just stay in your lane and do what I've taught you to do." Rivera won a scholarship to Ballanchine's school and went on to a famed Broadway career in "West Side Story" and "Chicago" among many other shows and to be the first Hispanic woman and first American Latina to receive the Kennedy Center honors award.**

The motivating leader inspires, pushes or perhaps pulls you to take action. She goes deeper than the surface impact of words to help you find your purpose or what Bill George (2015) calls your true north. This positive influence leader finds your "sweet spot;" that part of you that is central to who you are or who you are destined to become. It is not unusual for this leader to see that special something in you that even you have not yet realized was there. If you fail she will pick you back up, help you learn from your mistakes, and get you to see that success is still very much possible for you. However, she will also be completely honest with you providing the feedback that you need while, at the same time, showing you the path forward.

The motivating leader:

- sees that special something in you that might not have been apparent to you.

*Sarah L. Kaufman, "How Chita Rivera Keeps Dancing at 83, with 16 Screws in Her Leg," *Washington Post,* May 26, 2018

- helps you find your core purpose in life and work.
- provides you with the freedom to do the job without micro-managing, but remains accessible if you need help.
- believes that open and honest feedback is the key to personal growth.
- focuses on bringing out the best in members of his team rather than seeking to uncover their faults.
- helps people find their core strengths and then effectively utilize them.
- believes that resilience, persistence, and grit are the marks of people who are destined for success.
- provides you with a clear statement of the task or goal of the project, then gives you the freedom to figure out how to get it done.
- creates a team culture where the strengths of members are most effectively utilized.

Motivation is usually thought of as something that your boss (or coach or teacher or parent) does to get you to do something they want. Alternatively, many people believe lasting motivation comes from within the person and is based on the work.

In our view, a motivating positive influence manager:

1. sees something in you and helps you to see and accept it as well. Often, that special "something" is what you are destined to become.
2. helps you translate that "something" into a more practical core purpose or life/work goal.
3. operationalizes that core purpose by providing the resources and putting you in a position to be successful, to be your best self.
4. t a practical level encourages you to act independently while remaining accessible as a supportive resource.

She Sees Something in You

The effective motivating positive influence manager takes the time to understand you and look beneath to help you uncover that which you were destined to become. While you may think of yourself in a certain way or perhaps have trained to become a certain person, a creative manager comes along and sees something different. And that is often just what you need to help you get to a place where you say, "Yes, that's it, that's what I'm here for."

For example, Nancy, a senior-level manager with a major insurance company, was motivated by the actions of her first boss, Greg. He saw something in her that she had not yet realized was there. She shared with us:

> Greg would say to me, "You need to do this, you can do it." He gave me big, challenging projects, which developed my ability to execute. He has an ability to be accessible, but not hover. He also encouraged me to learn from others, but always said, "You figure it out, but I'll be available to help."
>
> It was clear that I could make mistakes (just not big ones) but he always helped me learn from them. He would say, "You screwed up—what did you learn?" All along the way he would support, push, but not hover while providing solid feedback on my performance.

Effective leaders motivate people who have doubts about their ability to get the work done or take on a new project. Esther, a multi-cultural marketing consultant, told us that when she was at AT&T her boss asked her to take on the major task of creating a national multi-cultural public relations department. When Esther expressed some reservations about it, he said, "Don't tell me you can't do it just because you never done it before. You have the right combination of smarts and experience to do it. Just go do it!"

As we discussed earlier, Betsy's college experience helped her find her true calling in the technical side of theater productions at a time when few women pursued this end of the business. And perhaps to her surprise she found that she liked and was good at things like lighting and set design. As a result, after college she landed a job on the technical staff of the famed Roundabout Theatre in New York City. However, once again, she ran smack up against an old-school technical director who did not like the idea of a woman working on the technical side of a production. When his opposition and the unnecessary barriers finally started to get Betsy down, she said to Rich, her significant other, "I don't think I can do this anymore." His response motivated her to continue and push back against the director. "Betsy, you have one of the best minds in the business. You can do it. Go back out there and show them." And she did.

In our research a consistent theme that we heard multiple times in the course of our interviews is that a positive influence was someone "who saw something in me that I did not see in myself and that others did not see in me." In fact, for the authors, this was central to the genesis of the book because someone early on in their work life saw something in them that resulted in a change in their career path.

Helps You Find Your Core Purpose

To be a positive influence you must get to know each person on your team, their personality, their work style, their concerns, and needs. This knowledge is essential if you are going to be able to motivate anyone to achieve great success.

Often it is a manager very early in your career who is that motivating positive influence. You encounter them at a time when you are not fully formed and, if you are open, ready to receive and utilize their perspective. They see that something in you and can help you find your core purpose, your true north. Such was the case with Nancy who cites Terry Taylor, her editor at the Associated Press, as a seminal force in her work life. As Nancy told us:

> Not only did Terry give me opportunities that made me realize that I wanted to be a sportswriter, but she set the tone in our department that women were every bit equal to men. I didn't realize it until later how valuable that was.

For Mindi, founder and director of a center for abused women, Mona was a life-altering motivating influence in her life and career. Early in Mindi's work life, Mona was her boss at a women's health clinic. At one point when Mindi expressed a desire to start a place for abused women:

> Mona said to her, "Why haven't you done it; sounds like a bunch of bullshit to me. You can come up with a bunch of excuses to

> not make it happen." I never forgot that conversation. It led me to get off my butt and do something about it.

Gissoo worked for 25 years in financial services until her brother died of cancer. She vowed to do something "so that no one else had to go through what he went through." She took a year off to think about cancer advocacy and perhaps work in the field. In the end she was able to get a job working for a large pharmaceutical company as "the voice of patients in the organization to ensure that the patient's voice is included early and often in the drug development process." She was fortunate to be able to interact with a very high-level executive in the company who was a motivating positive influence. His advice to Gissoo:

> "You can't boil the ocean. Do one thing and do it well." He gave me a long-term view of life, career, and work. He helped me focus my activities on the long-term aspects over the work I needed to get done now.

People can also be motivated by the courage you show in face of challenging circumstances. For example, in an extraordinary example of such courage, Peter, a medical oncologist we interviewed said, "I get inspiration from my patients as they are going through their treatments." He cited the example of a woman who was told by a famed cancer institute that "there was nothing they could do for her." She decided that she was going to live for one year to see her first son married but she also lived to see her second son married and for a total of 15 more years! Peter said, "I learned from her and others to be positive and to pass it along to my patients."

For Gina, now a nurse educator and assistant professor of psychiatric nursing, Debbie was that leader who was a motivating positive influence. As Gina told us:

> Debbie helped me find my pathways, to always put a positive spin on the negative. She challenged my negative thoughts and cognitive distortions. Her style was to help me deflect those thoughts using Socratic questions. She helped me investigate other avenues, deal with barriers and see other possibilities. The net result of her motivating influence is that I always think about what I'm doing.

Sometimes what a manager says has a motivating positive influence on you while in other situations it is their actions that are critical to your development. For example, Anne told us that Bob, a regional manager in her financial services company, saw her core strengths early on in her career. At the same time, he felt the company needed more women in senior roles. The confluence of those two things resulted in Anne's promotion to branch manager. In an interesting sidelight, Anne told us, "When I got the job two guys freaked out, but later became two of her biggest fans."

Another member of our study group, Dick, was quick to point out the motivating influence of Bill, his vice president of human resources during the critical period in his development. Dick said, "He got me focused, gave me a sense of meaning in my life and work." Bill never told Dick how to do his job, but he would often ask, "Have you thought through what you are about to do? What are the consequences of what you are about to do?" It was just these kinds of questions, and the conversations that they sparked that helped Dick shape his character, to develop an effective approach to people, and to have foresight into potential issues. "I learned," Dick said, "to take responsibility for my actions because I own my actions."

For most people, discovering their true north is essential to a successful and satisfying work life and career. If you are fortunate, you encounter a motivating positive influence leader early in your career who helps you discover your core purpose.

Positions You for Success

Simply finding your central purpose is the first step. Implementation requires a motivating manager who gives you confidence and resources and, importantly, puts you in spot where you will thrive.

Legendary airline entrepreneur Freddie Laker provided Virgin Atlantic founder, Richard Branson with both inspiration and practical advice that motivated him to go forward despite the intense competition that he faced from other airlines. Laker helped Bramson shape his vision of an airline that offered a quality experience at competitive prices.

Laker's down-to-earth wisdom was the force that made Branson decide that he should be the face of the company and to use the force of his slightly eccentric personality to gain free publicity for the airline thus off-setting the paucity of his advertising budget. Implementing this advice, Branson says he "found by standing out in fun and different ways, your chances of ending up on the front page of the newspaper, rather than the back, are much higher." (Coleman, August 10, 2016).

Jody was fortunate to work for Tom, a motivating manager, who was a very positive influence on her. It was his motivating leadership that led her to be confident enough to propose a very forward-looking human resources program. When her business unit was told by the FDA (Federal Drug Administration) to go back and do more testing—testing that would take several years to complete—Jody would have been required to layoff many people. However, she proposed instead that her human resources department become a "temp agency" that placed company employees with other business units during this time rather than lay them off. Despite the objections of numerous naysayers who said it would never work, she persisted, and it worked. Tom helped Jody uncover that special something in her that gave her the courage and resilience to succeed in face of opposition.

Ray, a senior-level IT manager and CIO at a number of global companies, had a benefit of several bosses who unlocked the key to motivating him to action. At W. R. Grace Europe, Jean-Louis saw in Ray the need for a major challenge and to be a central player in the change process that he was about to propose for the company. At the same time, someone was needed to break down the barriers, bring the UK folks onboard and get everyone supportive of Jean-Louis' vision of a united W. R. Grace Europe linked by computer systems. His leadership strategy was to first convince Ray of the logic of his vision but leave it to him to figure out the best way to get it done in the UK.

Motivating leaders create the conditions that increase the likelihood that you will succeed. They not only believe in you, but they take specific actions that position you to accomplish great things. At that point it's up to you to make it happen through your talent and your determination. For example, our rock musician, Rob, points to Mathew, who signed the band to a record contract and got their music out there in a caring and thoughtful way. His actions gave Rob the feeling that he believed in their music and this gave them great confidence that they were going to be successful. Rob said, in a most profound way, "Your music is better if you're confident." This is an important learning for a leader—when you give someone confidence, their work will be better and everyone benefits.

A truly involved parent can be an extremely motivating person if she also takes the time to know her son. One such mother is Tyneeha Rivers whose son is Mikal Bridges, a top-flight basketball player at Villanova University and a high draft selection of an NBA team in 2018. In addition to being a very good player, Bridges is seen as young man who works hard and has shown great improvement over the course of his career.

His character is shaped by his mother who said to him early in life, "Say what you want to be and say what you want to do and start taking steps to get there." Over the years her motivational strategy has not changed—set goals and work to accomplish them. "She also made sure he wasn't afraid of failure (she used to make him do ten pushups for every free throw missed) and that has translated into a player with work ethic and humility" (Adams, June 21, 2018).

Positioning can mean different things to different people, and it should. For some it may be the right job in the right organization while for others it may getting the right training and resources. It is the high-performing motivating manager who facilitates positive positioning.

Empowers You to Act

People learn and grow when they sense that their manager trusts them. And that trust is reflected in everyday actions when they are empowered to act and to make decisions about how and when the work gets done. However, empowerment is not abandonment. The effective motivating positive influence manager empowers her people but always makes it clear: "I've got your back or I'm here if you need me."

Frank, a manager we interviewed, said his first boss was that type of leader. "He got to know us and was, therefore, able to tailor his leadership style to each person and increase their effectiveness." Frank went on to say that his boss would often say, "look we all know what we have to do; so just go ahead and do it, but I'm here, if you need me, to get you more resources, deal with an obstacle or even talk with an uncooperative person."

Similarly, for Amy, she was fortunate to work for Ann, a new manager who recognized that while she brought extensive executive experience, she lacked subject-matter expertise. Ann was that motivating positive influence because, as Amy told us, "She used my ideas and experience, empowered me to do what was needed and, importantly, ensured I got credit for the work."

Debra shared with us that her boss, Sue, was a positive influence leader who motivated us all because "she was candid about the things she was struggling with." As a result, a work culture was created that gave us permission to share "soft stuff" and, therefore, participate, share and, above all, learn from each other. Most importantly, Debra said, "I always felt she had my back."

Similarly, Beth, an instructional designer, was motivated by her father, a corporate manager who motivated her to work hard. She told us, he was:

> Always the first at work in the morning and the last to leave at night. He was so charismatic that people loved him. I learned that to be a motivating positive influence you have to set an example by working hard, delegating to people, but staying involved with them by saying, "I'm here for you." He was always accessible but yet he insisted on people taking personal accountability for their work. As he said, "If you make a mistake, admit it and fix it... and always do the right thing."

Looking Back: Some Issues to Consider

As our research indicates, the motivating manager provides you with the freedom to do the job without micro-managing your work. However, empowerment does not mean abandonment. The effective motivating positive influence manager always remains accessible if you need her.

The motivating positive influence leader knows you well enough to sense your special calling that you may have not yet realized. She will help you discover your life's mission and put you in a situation where you can shine and then enable you to succeed on your own.

A Word about Legends

There are times when a person can be motivated by the positive influence of a legend as in the example of Bob Dylan and Woodie Guthrie (Callaway, May 24, 2013).

In the world of music one of the most famous influential relationships was the manner in which Bob Dylan was motivated by the life and music of Woody Guthrie. Guthrie, the singer-songwriter, was the author of perhaps the most famous folk song of all time, "This Land is Your Land." Dylan allegedly read Guthrie's autobiography, *Bound for Glory*, and became obsessed with him. Dylan, who is originally from Minnesota, started mimicking Guthrie's Oklahoman speech patterns set out in his book, and when he arrived in New York in 1961, he told a crowd at a club where he was performing, "I been travelling around the country, following in Woody Guthrie's footsteps."

Dylan went to visit Guthrie in Greystone Park Psychiatric Hospital where Guthrie was hospitalized with Huntington's disease. Dylan played a piece called *Song to Woody*, which Guthrie apparently approved of and appreciated. *Song to Woody* was released on Dylan's debut album, entitled *Bob Dylan*. Over 50 years later, it is still one of his best-known songs and one of the most famous tributes to the American folk tradition. In the song, Dylan uses language to share his view of Guthrie's life and combines it with a more personal style:

I'm seein' your world of people and things

Your paupers and peasants and princes and kings

Hey, Woody Guthrie, but I know that you know

All the things that I'm a-sayin' an' a-many times more

I'm a-singin' you the song, but I can't sing enough

'Cause there's not many men that done the things that you've done

1. There are several examples in this chapter of leaders sharing a harsh reality, a direct comment, or uncomfortable feedback with a person that ultimately served as a motivating positive influence for the person. Have you been given any similar feedback that you found to be uncomfortable at first but ultimately helpful?
2. Describe what someone did that helped you find your core purpose or true north.

3. Motivating leaders believe in you and your ability to do the job but go beyond that to create the conditions that position you for success. Drawing upon your experience, share some examples of what leaders have done to help you succeed.
4. A number of the people we interviewed said that their positive influence manager used the Socratic or questioning method to great success with them. Why is that methodology used by successful motivating positive influence managers? What has your experience been in using this process?

Chapter 6
The Role Model Leader

> *Oscar nominee Jessica Chastain says that, despite all the acclaim, she still doesn't feel totally confident or secure—but that's not a bad thing. She called French actress Isabelle Huppert a role model: "She's constantly challenging herself and doing theater. She puts herself in situations where: okay, we all know she's a genius and a brilliant actress, she could take the easy road right now. But she doesn't. She's always putting herself in a situation where she goes: 'I've never done this before. Let's see what happens.'"**

The role model leader can be a powerful force in a person's life and career. They provide an example from which you can learn how to be successful. You may choose to closely emulate a person you admire, although you may also benefit by extracting certain traits and integrating them with your unique style. If you are fortunate enough to spend time with your role model, he can share his experience in dealing with similar situations that you will face.

We are also aware of many people whose role model is someone they have admired from afar but never met. They learn by observing the person and researching how they handle various situations. For example, many of today's professional basketball players say that when they were young, Michael Jordan was their role model. Beyond his accomplishments, they admired and emulated his careful preparation, discipline, and singular focus.

The effective role model is very aware that words must be aligned with actions—walk the talk—because people you intend to influence are watching. It is axiomatic that if you want members of your team to provide high-quality customer service, then all of your customer interactions must meet that same elevated standard. Similarly, if you promote a culture of ethical behavior in your organization, it is critical that every time you interface with customers, team members, and stakeholders that you demonstrate a commensurate level of integrity.

*Fradkin, Sept. 13, 2013

The role model leader is a positive influence by articulating a clear vision and describing the path forward. They never foster a dependency relationship but rather empower people to seek and find their own destiny. They model a participative process because they know that "we are stronger together."

The role model leader is:

- a positive example of a person who has achieved success.
- a prototype of someone who does things the right way.
- a person who challenges you to find your own unique path to success.
- the type of leader who is easily accessible and approachable by people in the organization.
- the leader who urges you to think outside of the box.
- the manager who pushes you to seek goals that challenge your previously conceived limitations.
- a person who willingly shares her past missteps as a way of demonstrating that corrective action is possible.
- a leader who "walks the talks" and thus ensures her actions are always consistent with her words.
- that manager who demonstrates a positive work ethic by working longer and harder than anyone in the organization.
- a leader who is able to communicate a vision in such a compelling way that others want to follow.

Cook and Macaulay (2014, p.2) point out, "Role models are accessible examples of behavior and positive role modeling that encourage (positive) behaviors that lead to a more effective organization." All role models, however, are not the same. While some role models can be a negative force, in this context we are referring to role models who are a positive influence.

Four Types of Role Models

There are different types of role models with differing impacts on the actions of the people whom they influence. Gleaned from our interview data we have isolated four varieties of positive influence role models:

1. Inspirational
2. Game Changing
3. Motivating
4. Practical

The ***inspirational role model*** generates a positive response at an emotional level from the people they encounter. People are often "moved" at a very basic level by observing a specific role model.

The ***game-changing or life-altering role model*** is a powerful example of how to do things in the right way. By their example, they show a different way, an alternative path to success.

The ***motivating role model*** challenges you to change course or find a new approach to success. They often get you to test your previous assumptions and perhaps change your path.

The ***practical role model*** is just that—realistic, sensible, down-to-earth. Their actions are concrete and field-tested.

The Inspirational Role Model

As we said earlier, without ever having met them, Michael Jordan was an inspirational role model to a generation of basketball players in much the same way Marlon Brando was a role model to some of the finest actors of our time.

Similarly, Oprah Winfrey has served as a positive example for many people she has yet to meet. For example, here is an excerpt from a thank-you note sent to her:

> I come from a broken home. I have no brothers and sisters. I have never met my father and I recently found out my mother is a lesbian. The reason I am telling you this is because by seeing you handle your problems so well it makes me get through the hard times even though I don't know you. (Jensen, June 8, 2018).

Anne, a senior executive at CITI Group who we interviewed, said that Sallie Krawcheck was an inspiring role model when she was at Smith Barney. Krawcheck's career showed how it was possible for a woman to rise to the top in a predominantly male organization. Sallie was also a powerful example of, as Anne said, "It's OK to be a woman and a mom and still succeed on Wall Street."

As a way of reinforcing this conclusion Anne told us this story of an all-hands conference call that Sallie led. "She (Sallie) starts the call but then puts them on hold for 90 seconds. She comes back and says it was her four-year old daughter who could not find her pink nail polish and 'I told my daughter that I would always take her call.'"

Linda, a fitness instructor and manager at a major fitness and wellness center, pointed to her mother as an inspiring role model who, by her actions "gave me the strength to know that I will always be able to deal with things that come up in my life."

Linda's parents emigrated from Taiwan to the United States when she was 7 years old. Her mother was not happily married, and when Linda went to college, her mother moved to Los Angeles with nothing. She started selling jewelry in flea markets and eventually became the biggest gemstone dealer in California. As Linda told us, "She reinvented herself. It was so brave of her to do it. Asian women did not do that type of thing. She is my role model."

Frank, a psychiatrist we interviewed, said his father, a surgeon, was an inspiring role model and positive influence on him as he was growing up. Frank grew up listening to his father's stories about his work and how he treated the people he encountered. He taught Frank the importance of a strong moral center and a set of values about how to treat people with dignity and respect. In turn, Frank has passed along to his children "the importance of being respectful; we are all the same; all our stories are sacred."

Mindi's boss at the abortion clinic "wanted the clinic to be the Ritz-Carlton of clinics." As Mindi told us:

> Mona always greeted people at the door with "you are loved, you are safe." Despite the fact that the clinic had been fire bombed, nails put in staff's tires and had received numerous threatening messages, her people stayed with her for more than 20 years. Over the years she received many awards but always said, "This award belongs to my staff and volunteers."

Adrianna saw Dina, a deputy to the President's National Security Council, as a role model from whom she could learn that "preparation at all levels matters." Adrianna wants to make an impact on the world. And in Dina, Adrianna found someone to whom she could relate and see that it is possible to be an immigrant woman of global impact. This is the essence of an inspiring positive influence role model leader.

Hedge fund manager Mark said that one of his university professors was a role model from the standpoint of both his expertise and his interpersonal presence. He was the head of the economics department and author of several books. Mark called him a model of a "compassionate conservative." However, beyond his academic accomplishments:

> He loved to teach and would send private notes to his students and their parents. He took the time to reach out to people on a personal level while being a model of civility, truth and decency—something that's missing in society today. He didn't tinker his beliefs for anyone but was respectful to everyone and their views. He listened to their views and was never hostile or antagonistic.

Nelson Mandela was a positive role model for Barack Obama long before the two leaders met. When Obama was an undergraduate student at Occidental College he was inspired to get involved and participate in an anti-apartheid rally on campus.

Olympic Gold Medal winner Picabo Street was an inspirational, positive influence on American alpine ski champion Lindsey Vonn. When Lindsey was just nine years old, she met her idol, Street, an interaction that barely lasted two minutes but, Vonn says:

> She was the reason why I wanted to be an Olympic skier. She was larger than life. It's kind of like meeting a superhero and never thinking that they actually really exist until you meet them in person. She had this energy and charisma that you could feel, and it just kind of sucked me in. I was like, I'm in. I want to be you, whatever you did. I'm in.

Vonn, in fact, told *USA Today Sports* that "she still has the poster Street signed. 'Follow Your Dreams,' hanging in her bedroom back home in Colorado." Vonn, in turn, seeks to be an empowering role model to young girls who attend her Strong Girls Camp. Vonn wants to teach girls at a young age that they can achieve anything and not to think of themselves as "less than" whether it's about pay or performance, or both (Bromberg, August 19, 2019).

Similarly, Dominique Dawes, the first African American to win an Olympic gold medal in gymnastics, was an inspiring role model to Gabby Douglas. Douglas became the first African American to win gold in the women's gymnastics all-around competition. Dawes was happy to be a role model to Douglass and thrilled for her victory because she knows what it takes to compete and win Olympic competitions. She is also happy to have been a role model to other young girls of color who have similar aspirations. Now she is happy to turn that torch over to Gabby Douglas who will, in a similar vein, be a role model for future generations of young women (McFadden, August 3, 2012).

The Game-Changing Role Model

The highly successful businessman and former mayor of New York City Michael Bloomberg credits much of his success to the late William Solomon, managing partner at Solomon Brothers where Bloomberg started as a trader. Bloomberg says, "He taught by leading and he led by example. On most mornings, he'd be the first one in the office. He was a good listener but didn't manage by consensus. He was his own man, he made his own decisions and he didn't look back" (Entis, August 6, 2015). Bloomberg says those lessons were game changers because he took them with him when started his own company with three other former Solomon employees.

At Day 1 of the US Open Tennis Championships there was a powerful moment following the unveiling of the new statue of Althea Gibson, the first player of color, male or female, to play at the U.S. national tournament in 1950. Billie Jean King spoke at the ceremony calling Gibson "our Jackie Robinson."

> King met Gibson as a 15-year old in Los Angeles and said it was a life-changing moment because it taught her what a champion looks like. "That's the day I learned, if you can see it, you can be it." King, who so idolized Gibson she literally slept with a copy of her book, *I Always Wanted to Be Somebody* (Coffey, August 27, 2019).

Renowned instructional designer, workshop leader, and author Thiagi told us his father was a role model as a teacher and writer. However, his father, despite being a headmaster, teacher, and author of textbooks, did not want Thiagi to become a teacher. His father said to him, "Teaching is a thankless job."

However, Thiagi decided to become a teacher anyway because as he said:

> I liked the idea of trying to inspire people. In fact, all of my positive influences were teachers because they made a difference in students' lives because of their qualities. I wanted to prove my father wrong about teaching. And I did prove him wrong—teaching is not thankless.

Later when Thiagi came to the United States to continue his studies, he became a research assistant for Doug, a university professor. Doug became a role model in the way that he approached how people learn and, therefore, how you design learning for them. He learned from Doug:

> All people are smart in their own way. Never judge people by their differences. People are similar. The most important differences are the differences in the way they learn. There is a universality about human behavior. The learner should decide what to learn and how to learn it. Trust people to figure it out. There is no one single approach to learning.

Earlier in her career, Amy was fortunate to work for Evelyn in corporate social responsibility at a major pharmaceutical company. Evelyn was Amy's role model and a significant positive influence because she:

> Never micro-managed but always asked for and used my ideas. She listened and encouraged me to further develop myself. However, she backed up those words by sending me to development opportunities as well as professional association meetings and networking events. Her faith and trust in me and her willingness to empower me to take action gave me the confidence to be successful. Evelyn was a true role model and positive influence.

Ramon, a marathon runner, running coach, and senior manager with a large charity organization said his running coach was also a powerful role model because of his passion for the work. He gave Ramon his first opportunity as a coach, and he always tries to bring the same kind of enthusiasm and positive feeling to the runners he coaches. Ramon said, "I seek to be a role model myself because I never ask you to do something that I don't do, too. I never stop because I'm tired. I always bring high energy and a positive attitude."

Executive coach and author Stuart told us about Jim, his role model from whom he learned to "speak my truth." At first, he observed Jim saying things that Stuart might want to say, but never had the nerve to say. Stuart started logging the feelings and results when spoke the truth. Stuart said, the truth was always there. "Jim just gave me permission to let it out."

Another interviewee, Mark, a hedge fund manager graduated from Harvard Business School and went to work for AT&T, where his first manager was Richard. Richard's actions were a perfect example of how to treat people on the job.

> On my first day, I received a "welcome aboard" note, which also described the opportunity ahead of me. Although he guessed I might not be there long, he did not care and always included me in important meetings. Richard was a role model because he wasn't boastful, but very smart and humble. I watched him be inclusive and a great listener.

On the other hand, Tony, our martial arts instructor, saw a peer as a role model when he was a captain in the Marines. The officer had a personal code of ethics and was, at the same time, inspirational. It was the force of his example that led Tony to "stop shifting blame on to others, but rather accept it and own it." In an interesting twist on the influence of a role model, Tony said, "This captain's personal conduct made me feel morally defunct; this bothered me and so I became a better person as a result."

The Motivating Role Model

In a few situations we have found that a person can be a multi-layered positive influence in that they can both be a motivational force and a role model. For example, in the previous chapter, we said that Beth was motivated by her father when she had the opportunity to work with him as a high school student. He stimulated her interest in various aspects of computers that has informed her career.

However, her father was also an inspiring role model because he was always the first at work in the morning and the last to leave at night. She observed him delegating work to people on his team while remaining accessible to them when they encountered problems. She also saw that he insisted upon personal accountability.

Similarly, Dick, another corporate executive in our interview group, said that Bill was a motivational positive influence leader as an informal mentor who inspired Dick to take responsibility for his actions, especially in regard to how to treat people. However, Bill was also a very practical positive influence role model leader because Dick said, "I watched him every day and was especially impressed by the fact that he behaved the way he talked." As we said earlier in this chapter, people learn by watching to see if your words are supported by your actions. "Walking the talk" is a hallmark of an effective positive influence role model leader.

In her long career as a sportswriter, Nancy was fortunate to work for Terry Taylor at the Associated Press where she was both a supportive and motivating positive influence leader. While she gave Nancy the opportunities that made her realize she wanted to be a sportswriter she was also a major role model because, as Nancy shared with us:

> When you're a woman in a male-dominated industry, there are so many additional challenges. People question your ability as well as your motivations. People want to preserve the status quo. Seemingly trivial details, such as what you wear to work, take on added importance.

The Practical Role Model

In a slightly different take on the relationship between you and your role model and how they may have a positive influence on you, well-known financial advisor, author, and television host, Suze Orman says, "It's not about creating a cookie-cutter mold of yourself. Instead, the best mentors help their mentees find their own paths and succeed on their own terms" (Entis, August 6, 2015).

Orman is a mentor to personal trainer and television personality Jillian Michaels. Their relationship demonstrates this truth about how to be an effective positive influence role model leader. While the person may look up to and admire you, they should never feel the need to be exactly like you.

Similarly, TV and film star Melissa McCarthy believes that confidence was built into her DNA by her mother. McCarthy said, "I just didn't grow up worrying about keeping up with the Jones or what other people would think. My mom never delved into that sort of drama. If there was something that annoyed her, I didn't hear about it. She didn't give it time on her calendar. She is really solid in her shoes—she wishes people well and then keeps on moving. Watching that as an example is one the greatest gifts I got from her" (Coyne, May 21, 2018).

Ray, our senior level IT executive, saw his boss, Fred, as a role model but with a twist. Ray admired and wanted to adopt his style of being forthright about the desired goal. However, Ray also adapted that style to be more aligned with his inclusive personality. When Ray was working with the company's local management team in Chile, he approached them not with "my way or the highway" but with "how can I help you with your issues." Ray told us, "I was not dogmatic, but I always kept my eye on the end goal as set out by Fred."

Another one of our study group members, Jennifer, saw her boss as a practical role model. I admired and wanted to be like him because he created a "no nonsense" culture where the focus was on "work fast, never say no and innovate whenever possible." He also provided "very little day-to-day oversight, which gave me the freedom to lead my own group and grow as a manager."

Early in his career, Frank worked for Andy from whom he learned that "people have to take responsibility for their actions. More specifically:

> He set an example for people—he was the first one to work in the morning. He always "promoted" his people to senior management and his peers. He took the time to thank you for doing a good job. Importantly, he was a very good listener who took your point of view into consideration when making a decision. I looked to him for guidance and always wanted to emulate him. Andy was not a micro-manager. He was there for me but not on top of me. As he often said, "I'm going to tug on your rope and if I don't feel anything, I'm going to come looking for you."

Bob, a learning and development consultant and community activist we interviewed, said that Curt was a role model for him as a young African

American student in a college where the percentage of black students was 0.5 percent. Curt was an upper classman who helped Bob by getting him a job in the library but, beyond that, was someone who was "a role model for his steadiness, his rigor, discipline and from whom I learned how to position myself, how to speak and how to develop social skills."

Looking Back: Some Issues to Consider

A role model can be a positive influence who is close-up and very much a part of your life. A close-up role model who is a positive influence on you can be a parent, teacher, coach, friend, or manager. In this chapter we have representative examples of each category.

However, you may also be influenced by a role model who you have never met and probably never will. Marlon Brando, for example, inspired several generations of actors, including Jack Nicholson, Robert De Niro, and Al Pacino, early on, followed by Sean Penn, Johnny Depp, and Daniel-Day Lewis and, more recently, Christine Bale, Ryan Gosling, and James Franco (Piccalo, 2017). Beginning in the 1970s a generation of feminists were inspired by the actions of Gloria Steinem, Congresswoman Bella Abzug, and Congresswoman Shirley Chisholm to get involved in social activism and politics (Carmody, August 22, 1972).

Whether your role model is someone you know well or a person you have never met, they can have a significant impact on your personal and work life. They provide a standard to which you may aspire and against which you can measure yourself. Some people attempt to absorb the totality of their role model while others isolate specific, behavioral qualities and try to integrate them with their leadership style. For example, a basketball player may adopt Michael Jordan's work ethic but not try to emulate the style of his jump shot. An actor may embrace Marlon Brando's manner of preparing for a scene while not trying to imitate his manners and speech patterns.

Another critical component of the role model positive influence leader is alignment. A role model can only be a positive influence if there is always consistency between his words and his actions. As the saying goes, he always "walks the talk."

There are also different types of role models. The inspirational positive influence role model moves you at some basic level to take action while the game changer shows you another or perhaps an unconventional route to success. The motivating role model challenges you to take another look at your approach while the practical role model provides examples of the "nuts and bolts" of the avenues to a successful work life.

1. Who is your role model? Is it someone you know or is it someone you admire from afar? In what ways have they been a positive influence on your life and career?
2. Is it important that a role model be someone who has a similar background as you, e.g., gender, color, career?
3. What type of a role model are you? What do you do to be a positive influence role model on others—people you manage, people you coach, people you mentor?
4. What are some examples of positive influence role models in this chapter that resonated with you? Why?

Part 3

Helping People Become Their Best Self

Chapter 7
Profile of the Positive Influence Leader

*The relationship between Ralph Waldo Emerson and Henry David Thoreau and the positive influence each man had on the other has been well documented. Despite their differences—Emerson was fourteen years older and independently wealthy while Thoreau was a Harvard scholarship student—their relationship over the years impacted their writing. It has been said that Thoreau would not have devoted himself to and achieved success without the positive influence of Emerson. Emerson invited Thoreau to live with him during two different periods in his life, gave him work, lent him money, and encouraged him to build a cabin on the shore of Walden Pond, which resulted in his seminal work, Walden Pond or simply, Walden.**

We began with a simple belief that most everyone has a person in their life who was a positive influence. With that overarching premise our goal was to drill down to the essence of positive influence to identify the core characteristics of all positive influence leaders. The "drilling" involved a series of in-depth interviews in which we asked people to identify one or more persons who had a positive influence on them or in the vernacular "without this person I would not be where I am today."

In sports we often refer to such a person as a "game changer" or "difference maker." As you read this, it is quite natural to think, "Now, who would such a person be for me?" Alternatively, you may ask, "Am I a positive influence leader or do the members of my business team see me as a positive influence leader?" In fact, we encourage you to have that internal conversation as we move toward a profile of a positive influence leader.

After more than 50 interviews with a wide range of people, it has become clear that there is not one clearly-defined type of positive influence leader. There are many ways you can have a positive influence on a person you manage, a member of your team, or a colleague in the organization. Some may say that being a positive influence is a way of life.

*Smith, 1999

It's embedded in everything you do in every role you play in your life. It is how you parent, the manner in which you teach, how you coach your child's soccer team, the way you counsel a client, your work as a mentor, and how you lead an organization.

We have learned that there are four types or styles of positive influence leaders in much the same manner that Jung (1923) identified psychological types. We have a view of the four styles that says:

1. You have a predominant style that exhibits certain characteristics that you share with other people who also identify with that style. However, there will be a variation in the scope and depth of how each person makes use of their style in the workplace. These are no cookie-cutter styles.
2. Each of us has the capability to use the strengths of all four styles. However, we simply use one or two more often than the others. We refer to that style as your primary style.
3. Since we have within us the capacity to use all four styles, the most effective positive influence leaders can tailor their approach to each individual and, therefore, may use one style with one person and another style with another person.
4. Your predominant style or style configuration can change. Change can be self-directed, or it can a reaction to pressures to change from others. Survey feedback data provided by teammates and other colleagues (360° feedback) often provide a positive impetus to change as well.

Our research tells us that each of the four styles can be an effective positive influence leader but in different ways. The supportive leader believes in you and, more importantly, gets you to believe in yourself. On the other hand, the teacher leader will equip you with the things you need to learn in order to be successful but also encourage you to use those skills to succeed at the highest levels. The motivating leader inspires you to look inside yourself to find that special something or untapped part of you that will be life-altering. By contrast you look outside to find positive influence from a role model leader who serves as an example of how to do things "the right way."

Specifically, the supportive leader, for example, makes you believe you can be a successful first-time project leader of a new acquisition integration team. With skills and knowledge provided by the teacher leader, you agree to assume the role of relationship manager tasked with developing positive connections with the local management team of a new acquisition in Brazil. A motivating leader pushes you to see that your "true north" lies not with continuing as senior web developer but as a marketing manager with the integration team that is on-site with the recent acquisition in Brazil. Prior to your promotion to group supervisor, a role model leader emphasizes the importance of a close alignment between what you do and what you say as you work side by side with the local Brazilian management team.

One Predominant Style

As we have said, *there are four types of positive influence leader, and you can be an effective positive influence leader with any one of them as your predominant style*. You bring to the relationship certain strengths that will have a positive impact on the people you lead. The goal is to exploit those strengths while avoiding the tendency to use them to an excess or to a point where they become "too much of a good thing." For example, as a supportive leader you may have a tendency to be overly encouraging of a team member's current work situation at a time when the person may need to be motivated to chart a new career path.

At the same time, it is important to recognize that a member of your team may need a type of positive influence that is outside of your wheelhouse. When you are an especially strong positive influence leader with a definitive style, it may be challenging for you to use the strengths of another style. It is not unusual for a role model positive influence leader to rely on members of their business unit to learn by observing how they handle certain situations and specific people. However, some people learn best, or at least better, from a leader who is an effective teacher of the skills necessary to handle their current workplace challenges.

1. **The Supportive Positive Influence Leader helps people believe in themselves.** You believe in the people on your team and help each one of them believe in their ability to do the job and do it extremely well. The people on your team see you as credible with a high degree of integrity, such that your words "you can do this" have a ring of authenticity. Your leadership influence extends beyond individuals to your team. You reinforce the team's belief in their ability to solve a complex problem, develop a plan to address a challenging issue, or encourage members to collaborate on a cross-functional and multi-national basis.

Helpful Actions	Potential Downside
Make it clear you believe their goal is achievable	Overly optimistic
Indicate that they have it in themselves to be successful	Too shortsighted
Coach people to be able to handle things on their own	Unrealistic personal assessments
Help people see that they have choices	Failure to recognize obstacles
Provide encouragement that is authentic	Insufficient practical advice

2. **The Teacher Positive Influence Leader teaches people things they need to learn.** You are someone who carries the title of teacher or professor or perhaps, learning consultant, but more often you are simply a leader who is committed to teaching people the key success skills. You are that special person who creates in the members of your team the desire to learn and develop as key ingredients in their goal of being an accomplished person. As has been said "Success is preparation plus opportunity." Therefore, developing the necessary skills and acquiring the requisite knowledge positions the people you influence to take advantage of that important opportunity when it comes their way. The teacher positive influence leader is the facilitator of that process. In addition, the most effective positive influence leader will share their view of the realities and challenges of the world of work and ways to adapt to or work around the obstacles.

Helpful Actions	Potential Downside
Inspire a desire to learn	Information overload
Make the learning relevant	Too little hands-on learning
Identify teachable moments	Doesn't build on existing skills
Create learning on demand	Not relevant to the real world
Make learning fun	Fails to foster creativity

3. **The Motivating Positive Influence Leader inspires people to take action.** You are that leader who inspires people to take action. You find that special something in a person, maybe even something they are not in touch with, that will be a difference maker for them. You may be the person who pushes them to make a career change or return for additional training or apply for a promotion that seemed beyond their reach. You are the type of positive influence who is there when a person has a set-back, needs to learn from the experience, and get back on the road to success. You believe that failure is not the opposite of success but rather a step on the journey to success. You are an expert at delivering the truth in a way that it is heard and can be integrated into a positive development plan.

Helpful Actions	Potential Downside
Sees that special something in a person	Pushes too soon or too fast
Helps you find your core purpose	Micro-manages
Provides helpful feedback	Feedback is too tough or not timely
Remains available and accessible	Allows mistakes to go on too long
Empowers people to act	Delegates and disappears

4. **The Role Model Positive Influence Leader provides an example of how to succeed.** As a role model, you are a powerful force in a person's life and work experience. You are someone who people perceive as an example of how to prepare yourself for success. While they may not adopt all your specific qualities, they often profit from incorporating some of your traits and work habits. While you encourage members of your business unit to learn from your experience, you make it clear that it is critical that they create a unique work style that fits their personality, skills, and life goals. As a role model for people in your organization, you recognize the importance of alignment between your actions and your words. Alignment is the essence of integrity for a role model because people are always paying close attention.

Helpful Actions	Potential Downside
Serves as a positive example	Too remote
Provides a challenge	Traits seem too difficult to emulate
Shares failures and lessons learned	Experience does not seem relevant
Words and deeds are aligned	Process is out of date
Communicates a positive vision	Actions inconsistent with words

Two Predominant Styles

You can be an effective positive influence leader with two primary styles. In fact, *your ability to use the strengths of two different styles expands your options such that you are better positioned to be an effective positive influence leader than a leader with one primary style.*

You have a broader, more varied approach to your leadership of the people in your organization. If you can be both supportive and motivating or both a teacher and a role model, then you have the opportunity to be a more impactful positive influence than a leader who is only supportive. However, you are still prone to overusing your strengths in much the same way you do if you have one primary style. Since you are missing the strengths of two styles, you are not as effective in using some of the strengths associated with one of the other two styles. It may be that those strengths are just what is needed by a member of your team at that time.

1. **The Supportive Positive Influence Leader and the Teacher Positive Influence Leader.** You are the leader who both encourages people to believe in themselves while teaching them the skills they need to be successful. For example, Shirnette said her grandmother was the central figure in her upbringing as a young person. She both believed in her ability and taught her key skills such as how to read and write. Beth pointed to her father as that leader who both believed in her personally and professionally and taught her key technical skills such as how to program.

   People in your business unit will find your supportive and teacher positive influence leadership a real asset. However, your focus on these areas may mean that you fail to push people to move beyond their initial career choice to seek a challenge that will become their true destiny and central purpose in life. In addition, you may not be that role model, that powerful force from whom people on your team can benefit by observing how you effectively handle life's challenges.

2. **The Supportive Positive Influence Leader and the Motivating Positive Influence Leader.** You are that positive influence leader who combines the ability to instill a belief in a person that whatever goal is on their horizon they can achieve it with a leadership style that inspires a person to find and act on their true purpose in life. You bolster a person's sense that they can be successful, with an ability to push a person just enough so they can be their best self.

   Gina was told by a psychologist that "you can do it" and also helped her investigate other pathways and see possibilities. For Gina this person was, at the same time, supportive—"you got this" and motivating—"she saw something special in me."

   When there is alignment between being both a supportive leader and a motivating positive influence leader, you coach the person to the point where they can handle situations on their own and motivate them to get in touch with their core strengths and then use them effectively.

3. **The Supportive Positive Influence Leader and the Role Model Positive Influence Leader.** Since you combine the strengths of the supportive leader with the strengths of the role model leader this means that you have the ability to encourage the person to emulate their role model or, at the very least, adopt some of their strengths. Role models are often remote figures who may not be easily accessible, but your considerable encouragement will push a person to seek out and take advantage of their strengths.

   Dick told us that Bill, his manager of human resources, believed in him and thus supported his development as an HR professional. However, Bill was also a role model—Dick was able to observe him close-up on a daily basis—and he saw that Bill "behaved the way he talked." He was authentic.

   Earlier we mentioned Paul Gauguin who encouraged Van Gogh to bring his imagination into play when painting. However, Gauguin was also a role model for Van Gogh, who was anxious to become a famous impressionist artist like Gauguin.

4. **The Teacher Positive Influence Leader and the Motivating Positive Influence Leader.** With these two strengths you can both create a desire in a person to learn and then push them to use their skills to take positive action. You have that rare ability to impart to others the knowledge they need to be successful while also motivate them to learn from their mistakes and get back on their path forward.

   For example, Leslie, a woman we interviewed, talked about a professor who was the type of positive influence leader who taught her the practical things she needed to know while motivating her to become a great teacher—something she has become. Similarly, Danny pointed to Susan as someone who taught him sales techniques, but also "held me accountable and lit a fire in me" that pushed me to be great at my job.

   As a motivating positive influence leader, you often help people find their core strengths while the teacher positive influence side of you helps people make effective use of their core strengths by developing a repertoire of practical skills.

5. **The Teacher Positive Influence Leader and the Role Model Positive Influence Leader.** You provide people in your workplace with an example of how to achieve success while at the same time you can create a desire to learn and develop the expertise required to be an accomplished person who is admired by others. You are a positive influence who is able to present a compelling vision and the path forward to that end state, but you also help people learn the skills necessary to complete the tasks that get the team to that successful outcome.

   Renowned instructional designer and game developer Thiagi told us that Doug was both a great teacher and a role model for him. "He taught me to listen and to treat people with respect. All people are smart in their own way. They just learn in different ways."

   You are a prototype of someone who does things the right way and who teaches people to do things the right way. Some people can learn by simply observing how their role model does things while others need to be taught or at least motivated to learn how to do it the right way.

6. **The Motivating Positive Influence Leader and the Role Model Positive Influence Leader.** You are a leader who is able to both inspire people in your organization to take action while, at the same time, being a positive example from whom they learn. You can be a powerful leadership force because people often try to emulate your approach to life and work but may need to be motivated to take action in order to succeed. You are more of an activist leader for people on your team because you model a way forward to their best self while also pushing them to move forward toward their life goal.

   Jennifer's boss at the Smithsonian was a role model for her because he created a "no nonsense culture." However, his leadership style, which included very little direct oversight, also "motivated me to innovate; to take reasonable risks in search of a better way." It was his leadership style that combined motivating people to take action while serving as a forceful example of doing things the right way for the benefit of the museum's visitors.

Three Predominant Styles

If you have three primary styles, you have a wide range of strengths. *You have greater flexibility to employ a variety of actions with the members of your team depending upon their individual needs at any given time.* However, you will want to look at the one piece of the positive influence leader puzzle that is missing. Shoring up your strengths in the one missing area will increase your overall effectiveness as a positive influence leader.

1. **The Teacher Positive Influence Leader, the Motivating Positive Influence Leader, and the Role Model Positive Influence Leader.** While you have considerable strengths in these three areas as a leader, your strengths as a supportive leader are less effective. This means that you may need to work to improve your ability to be encouraging, to help people on your team believe they can be successful, and to make it clear that they have your backing.

2. **The Supportive Positive Influence Leader, the Motivating Positive Influence Leader, and the Role Model Positive Influence Leader.** You have a wide range of positive influence strengths as a supportive, motivating and role model leader but you lack a similar array of strengths as a teacher leader. The implications of this are that you need to upgrade in such areas as creating a desire to learn, teaching the relevant skills and knowledge to people in your organization, as well as prepare them for the challenges they will face in the future.

3. **The Supportive Positive Influence Leader, the Teacher Positive Influence Leader, and Role Model Positive Influence Leader.** You have a formidable assortment of positive influence tools at your disposal; however, your strengths as a motivator do not measure up to the other areas. As a result, you should consider improving your ability to inspire people to take action, especially in regard to finding their central purpose in life, helping them learn from their mistakes, and get back on the forward path to success.

4. **The Supportive Positive Influence Leader, the Teacher Positive Influence Leader, and the Motivating Positive Influence Leader.** You have an impressive collection of positive influence strengths as a supportive, teacher and motivating leader, but you lack a similar level of strength as a role model from whom others can

learn. Accordingly, you will need to realize that all that you do can have an impact on the members of your team and, therefore, you must make yourself accessible so that people can learn by observing what you do, how you handle situations and, most important, ensuring that your actions are closely aligned with your words.

Four Predominant Styles: The Transformational Positive Influence Leader

If you have four predominant styles—a uniform pattern of style distribution—you have maximum flexibility in your interactions with people in your organization. *You are able to easily provide a person with the type of leadership influence that is needed exactly when they need it.*

If, for example, someone needs supportive influence, you can be right there to provide it. ("You got this.") When a team member requires that you teach them important practical skills, you can easily provide the skills or information they need at the very moment they need it. ("Learn this now.") On the other hand, if someone needs a push to action or career direction, you have the insight to see that special something in them that will be life altering ("your core purpose"). And finally, you can be a powerful example from whom people in your organization can learn how to be successful ("my role model").

We believe that the very best of this type of leadership style is *situational*—providing each person just the right type of influence leadership at the very moment and place when they can make most effective use of it. It is the ultimate in leadership insight and action. *It is reasonable to call this person the transformational positive influence leader for our time.*

What's Your Style?

You can determine your style by completing the *Parker Positive Influence Leader Survey: A Self-Assessment* found in the Tools for Becoming a Positive Influence Leader Section.

Looking Back: Some Issues to Consider

1. What specific type or style of positive influence leader are you?
2. What are your strengths as a positive influence leader?
3. In what ways do you need to improve or expand your strengths?
4. Do you believe a person can be an effective positive influence leader with one predominant style?

Chapter 8
Pay It Forward

> *Benjamin Franklin first tried to popularize the concept of "pay it forward" when he wrote to a man who asked for a loan and said, "I only lend it to you. When you meet another honest man in similar distress, you must pay me by lending this sum to him; enjoining him to discharge the debt by a like operation. This is a trick of mine for doing a deal of good with a little money.**

People who have benefited from a positive influence in their life tend to be a positive force in the lives of people they encounter. They learn from their personal experience the importance and value of:

- supporting people who need confidence or encouragement to move forward toward their goals.
- teaching people the skills they need or instilling the values necessary for their journey.
- motivating people to find their core purpose and bring out the best in them.
- being a role model who provides a positive example of how to achieve success.

Our research indicates that some people take their experience of being on the receiving end of a positive influence leader and look for opportunities to have a similar impact on people they encounter in their work life. They can point to specific people they have impacted and the positive outcomes of those encounters. We also found that others have adopted a generalized approach to people that seeks to have a positive influence on everyone in their orbit. Their impact is limited only by those people who are not open to the receipt of any external influence. It is worth noting here that people who seek to influence others must first be open to being influenced themselves.

*Franklin (2017)

The people we interviewed were able to influence others because first they were open to and were positively influenced by others (Covey, Jan. 1995). In this chapter, we provide examples of both types—leaders who can point to the ways they influenced specific people and others who take a broader, less specific approach to being a positive influence.

Paying It Forward with a Specific Person

Many of today's celebrities pay it forward with major donations to existing charities, while some also help specific people. For example, Taylor Swift donated $1 million to the V Foundation for Cancer Research. However, she also gave $50,000 dollars to a fan battling cancer and a similar amount to the nephew of one of her backup dancers who is also being treated for cancer. Some famous people like singer John Legend establish their own foundation. Legend's Show Me Foundation provides funds to give poor children access to quality education. However, his wife, model Chrissy Teigen, recently gave $5,000 to a fan so she could attend beauty school.

Nurse educator Gina benefited greatly from a teacher who was a very supportive, positive influence leader in her doctoral nursing program. Gina, in turn, pays it forward in her work with disadvantaged, minority nursing students. She pointed to a specific student who was having great difficulty passing a course but would not ask for help. As Gina put it, she was "over-efforting" to compensate. Gina stepped in and talked to her professor about a work project in the student's neighborhood in lieu of a test for the course. It was more than just a happy ending in regard to the course because the student also learned that it was okay to ask for specific help.

Leslie, who teaches journalism to high school students, had a special relationship with Raul, a student she followed from tenth grade through his senior year. Raul had a passion for writing, something that Leslie supported and encouraged in her many conversations with him over the years as she continued to help him refine his skills. Later, he reached out to her, thanking her for the role she played in developing his writing and journalism skills. At the time, he was a speechwriter for President Barack Obama.

Debra, a senior manager in a large pharmaceutical company, benefited from several women early in her career who were a positive influence by helping her become more self-aware and focused on her successes while still dealing with areas that needed improvement. In turn, she has been a positive influence on a specific direct report in her organization—a woman who told her:

> You gave me an opportunity to grow, to see beyond my current self and, most important, to learn that you do not lose when you collaborate with others.

Tony, our martial arts instructor, made a conscious effort to pay it forward by volunteering at a rape crisis center where he taught martial arts to women, half of whom had been raped. He taught them the necessary skills to defend themselves but first, he said, "I had to break down their socialization tendencies. For example, when I hit them, they showed paralyzing emotional distress, sometimes including tears." However, he knew he was making progress when in a sparring match, he hit a woman a bit too hard and knocked her unconscious. As he knelt down to tend to her, she quickly regained consciousness and, immediately upon seeing him hovering over her, punched him in the nose. Tony told us, "It was the best reaction I could have hoped for."

Amy, a foundation executive, needed confidence early in her career and was fortunate to have a manager who was willing to share her expertise while listening to and using Amy's ideas and suggestions for organizational improvement. Empowering Amy gave her the confidence to grow as a person. Now, Amy is able to do something similar with college students she mentors. Specifically, she focused on one student who needed to learn the importance of effective communication along with a variety of workplace values such as timeliness. It was clear that taking an interest in the student helped her grow as a person.

As we said, sometimes it is a matter of giving someone the confidence to move forward, to expand their horizons, to seek out or augment their core purpose. For example, Beth, a learning consultant and instructional designer we interviewed, told us about her business partner. With patience and empathy, Beth worked to give her the confidence to move beyond her comfort zone and try something new. Such a strategy only works if the other person senses that you are a person of integrity and your actions are sincere. Excessive "rah-rah" motivational speeches fall flat in such situations.

At other times you need to be a positive influence teacher leader as, for instance, when Frank helped a member of his IT staff who was perceived by others in the user community to have "a chip on his shoulder." In digging into the situation, Frank found that the man became defensive and overreacted to criticism from IT users. Frank coached him by providing a series of tips on how to handle feedback without getting defensive. The key to success was that Frank did not intervene with the users but rather let the IT specialist handle the situations as they came up, thus giving him both the skills and confidence to grow as a professional. Frank's overarching message:

> You have the technical skills to do the job, and I know you have the ability to improve the relationship management skills that are critical to being a successful professional.

Shirnette, a radiation oncologist who benefited from a very positive influence in her early life, told us about a cancer patient whose mother and two sisters also had cancer. After the mother and sisters died, the patient became distraught and very worried that her cancer would return and she would die, too. In the meantime, her daughter died suddenly leaving three teenage children in her care. The woman was about to apply for food stamps when Shirnette began a drive in the Cancer Center to sponsor the family. This involved collecting money, clothing, and food and because it was near Christmas, presents. The employees found out what the children liked and what they needed. The staff delivered everything to the family who were greatly surprised and moved by the generosity of the staff. One of the three daughters, a psychology student, was so moved that she switched her major to nursing telling them that she wanted to become an oncology nurse because of what the nurses had done for her family.

Shirnette told us:

> I continue to see this patient for follow-up visits where I spend a great deal of time counseling her because she is still afraid that the cancer will return. On the other hand, I also see a smile on her face during these follow-up appointments. The woman calls the office periodically just to chat and the staff always takes the time to comfort her because they are aware of her fragile situation.

Esther, a multicultural marketing consultant who early on doubted herself, benefited from a motivating positive influence manager who told her she could do it even if she had never done it before. He said to her, "Just go do it." Esther brings that same positive influence leadership to the people she manages. One such person is a young man she hired with experience in the arts but little experience in government. She said, "I saw something in him." He took that opportunity and ran with it with the result that he now leads the corporate social responsibility function at a major global company.

Bob, our organizational development consultant, facilitated a strategic planning retreat for Caesar, the company's country manager in China. He wanted to increase his business. Bob worked with Caesar to develop the theme for the event: "212 degrees: just do a little more." He explained: "At 211 degrees, it's hot, at 212 it's boiling. So, no matter how much I think I know what to expect, there's always more."

Ray, a senior level corporate CIO, was a great influence on a junior analyst who worked for him. Later, the analyst became a CIO himself at a major company. When he had a decision to make, he told Ray, "I say to myself, what would Barratt do?"

Similarly, financial services executive, Anne, told us she was a positive influence on another Anne, a manager in her office, who, when confronted with a tough choice, asked herself, "What would Anne do in this situation?"

Executive recruiter Danny had a positive impact on Jordan when Danny was struggling professionally. Danny was able to "teach him the importance of ethics, taking an interest in people, hard work, commitment, professionalism and treating people with respect."

HR executive Jody served as a role model for Elaine because of her extraordinary work ethic. Jody told us:

> I helped build her confidence as a speaker, especially presenting her ideas clearly. I also helped her prepare for job interviews telling her, "Make sure you are interviewing them, too."

Sometimes you can pay it forward by being a mentor. For example, Bob, an OD and training consultant and a community activist, worked with Gail, a leader in the Columbia Heights community of the District of

Columbia. Bob told us, "Gail came to me with a general idea about starting a youth group in her community." Bob helped her start the Columbia Heights Youth Club and then stayed on as a mentor to share his ideas and help Gail work through issues that arise.

Paying It Forward Across the Board

All-star basketball player Lebron James is paying it forward in a big way to at-risk students in the Akron school system with his I Promise School. The school is creating a support system for the kids because James benefited from the support of several families who took an interest in him in the fourth grade. James missed 83 days of school in the fourth grade because he lived on the other side of town and had great difficulty getting back and forth from school. His fortunes changed when several families took him in and provided the positive influence support he needed to succeed in school. The I Promise School will provide a high level of quality support for the students, including, breakfast, lunch, and a snack. James said, "Fueling the body keeps the mind sharp" (McMenamin, July 31, 2018).

During his travels to Africa, actor Matt Damon learned about the challenges of providing access to safe water and sanitation in Saharan Africa. To address the issue, he co-founded www.water.org. Damon and his team have already raised more than $14 million to address the problem. However, he also takes an active interest in the work, including site visits to multiple countries, developing strategy and serving as an advocate for clean water in meetings with the World Bank and World Economic Forum.

Some people in our study group said they pay it forward by adopting the principles learned from their positive influence leader and applying them in all of their interactions. For example, Dick reported that he incorporates the teachings of his two main mentors—be present, focus on the person, be consistent in your actions and, above all, use a questioning mode of interpersonal interactions—in all of his efforts to be a positive influence on the people in his organization.

Similarly, Nancy, our senior-level HR manager in the insurance industry, applies the principles she learned from her major positive influence leader to all of her direct reports. For example, she listens to their concerns, doesn't jump in immediately with an answer, but rather encourages them to figure things out on their own. However, she remains easily accessible to them in case they need help along the way. In addition, she also emphasizes the importance of "showcasing" the people on her team, including pushing them into the spotlight whenever possible.

Mark has a principle that guides all his interactions with the people who work for him: "If you want to be a good boss, take more of the blame than you think you deserve and take less of the credit than you think you earned."

Similarly, Gissoo, a patient advocacy specialist for a pharmaceutical company, does both. She applies the principles she learned and adopted from a positive influence leader in the organization to all people she encounters. However, she also reported on a number of specific people she worked with in the organization where she was able to further their career using the methodologies she learned from her mentor. For example:

> A young man wanted to change jobs after only 18 months in his current position. Gissoo encouraged him to slow down while he grew his skills and, most important, took the time to meet key people across the organization, a process facilitated by Gissoo. He wanted to transition to sales, so Gissoo connected him with the head of field sales so he could ride with an experienced salesperson. Now, he is a vice president at another company in the industry.

Mindi, the founder and director of a community-based program for survivors of sexual abuse, helps all women there who have experienced trauma. Mindi survived sexual abuse and drug addiction but turned her life around with the support of her positive influence leader. She, in turn, especially helps rural women who come to the center with low self-esteem and lots of negative self-talk. ("I can't do this.") Mindi patiently moves them forward by encouraging them to make phone calls, give speeches, and write articles but, Mindi says, "I will be there with you all the way." Some have left the center, found employment, gained confidence, and become empowered women.

Betsy benefited from several people in the early part of her life who were supportive and believed in her, even when she doubted herself or when others doubted her. As a result, she passes this belief on to the people she supervises as she helps them realize they have skills that are not apparent to them or they do not have the confidence to utilize. Betsy is able to individualize her support of people by making it all about them and not what they can do for her.

Legendary instructional designer Thiagi has influenced a generation of workshop developers and facilitators with sacred learning nuggets such as:

- "Keep the process, change the content."
- "Make it up as you go along. Build the airplane while you are flying it."
- "The less the trainer talks, the more the learner will learn."

Frank, a psychiatrist we interviewed, learned the importance of morality and positive values from his father. He, in turn, passes these values along to his children and other people he encounters. Frank believes strongly in the value of treating all people with dignity, doing things the right way, and having a strong moral center. He told us, "I pass along the importance of being respectful, that we are all the same and all our stories are sacred."

Peter was enriched by a number of positive mentors during his early years as a student in the United States. He gained confidence from them, but also learned the importance of a positive attitude. He said, "I learned that you create your own barriers and, as a result, you need to also break down those barriers." Peter, an oncologist, always maintains a positive attitude with his patients, telling them stories of patients with a positive outlook, the benefits of setting a goal, being open to experimental approaches, and to think outside of the box.

Peter is also a mentor to medical school students and interns. Beyond the medical education, he emphasizes the importance of emotional intelligence including carefully listening to the patient, projecting a positive attitude, and taking the time to clearly explain things.

For years, the group New York Says Thank You has been traveling around the country helping people in areas hit by natural disasters. Every September the group travels to different areas that need help, typically rebuilding homes, as a way of saying "thank you" to all the people who aided New Yorkers after the attacks of September 11, 2001. In a great example of paying it forward many of those helped by the group later travel to other areas to volunteer with New York Says Thank You to help people hit by disasters. For example, after Superstorm Sandy, the group, at least half of whom were from outside the New York area, helped rebuild homes destroyed or severely damaged by the storm. Being a positive influence is contagious (Toner, September 13, 2013).

Looking Back: Some Issues to Consider

The people we interviewed were a positive influence on people they encountered in a random manner rather than as part of a conscious plan. It was not as if they deliberately helped the next person because they were helped; it just came naturally to them. And while all our interviewees found it easy to identify a person (often more than one) who was a positive influence on them, some had difficulty thinking of someone upon whom they were a positive influence. We believe some were just too modest to think they had a positive impact on another person.

The concept of pay it forward has come a long way since the days of Benjamin Franklin. The term was used in the 1951 book, *Between Planets*, by Robert A. Heinlein. Heinlein's work took the concept from an informal relationship between people to the formation of The Heinlein Society (*www.heinleinsociety.org*), a humanitarian organization that organizes blood drives, provides scholarships, and sends books to veterans and active military.

Another book, *Pay it Forward* (2000) resulted in a major film and the Pay it Forward Foundation (*www.payitforwardfoundation.org*) founded by the book's author, Catherine Ryan Hyde. The foundation encourages acts of kindness toward people, animals, and the planet.

1. In the course of your work life have you had the opportunity to be a positive influence on another person? Describe the situation.
2. Have you ever done a random act of kindness for a stranger? Why? What was the person's reaction?
3. Do you believe that people who have been on the receiving end of positive influence tend to be more likely to pay it forward? Why?
4. One member of our study group, an oncologist, learned the importance of maintaining a positive attitude during treatment from his patients. In your work life, what positive lesson that you have learned do you pass along to the people you encounter?

Chapter 9
Turning a Negative Influence Into a Positive Force

> *Zane Grey, who wrote ninety books that sold some 50 million copies, faced multiple rejections of his first manuscripts. One editor told him, "I do not see anything in this to convince me you can write either narrative or fiction." Yet Grey persevered, believing he had stories to tell about the American West that people would want to read.**

All of us are, by nature, social beings. We believe our happiness is a function of the quality of our relationships. We care about the people in our orbit and what they think of us. We want them to like us and to like what we do—our choices, our career, our friends, our opinions, our dreams. Solitary confinement is considered an extreme form of punishment because it takes away the opportunity to develop and maintain positive relationships.

You are indeed fortunate if all or most of the people in your life are positive influences.

- You were told at a young age "you can do it" the first time you hopped on a two-wheel bike, auditioned for the school orchestra, tried out for the field hockey team, or stood up to the neighborhood bully.
- You encountered someone who created a desire to learn, helped you fashion a set of positive values and ethical standards, taught you the relevant life skills or instilled a belief in you that failure is just a step on life's journey.
- At a key point in your life someone saw something in you that was not readily apparent to you, suggested a new career direction or life purpose, provided you with helpful feedback, or pushed you to make better use of your strengths.

**https://www.authors.me/best-selling-authors-who-were-rejected/*

- You met or saw someone who became a role model that you wanted to emulate, who showed you the path to success, taught you to how to overcome certain obstacles, or challenged you to be your best self.

The Forces of Negativity are Everywhere

Unfortunately, we all encounter people who seek (sometimes unknowingly) to bring us down with their negativity in the name of:

- "I'm just trying to be realistic."
- "I only want to give you the benefit of my experience."
- "It's a long shot."
- "That's not a career for a woman."
- "Only a few people make it in that field."

Sure, you can sometimes just walk away from such people, but it's not always possible when the person is your father, a brother, your boss, or your spouse. In many cases the intentions of these negative people in your life are good. They want the best for you, and, therefore, from their perspective it makes sense to question the validity of your choices because bad things may happen to you.

Our research indicates that the negative force can be a parent who says, "What are you going to do with a history degree?" While they truly worry that you won't be able to get job after you graduate, they don't realize that history majors usually find work in such fields as museum curator, secondary school teacher, journalist, geographer, research analyst...the list goes on...and with pretty good starting salaries. The question also misses the point of the passion that you bring to something that you truly love and at which you are willing to work tirelessly to achieve success. Remember our rock singer Rob, whose parents encouraged him to pursue his love of music and dream of becoming a successful rock musician.

Negativity can come from a manager early on in your corporate career whose controlling leadership style will try to discourage you from applying for that job opening in field sales. When he says, "Stay here in production engineering. Wait your turn and good things will happen for you," he is, perhaps unknowingly, both stifling your dreams and failing to see how your technical expertise can be a real asset in sales.

What you also have here is a manager imposing his own tendency to risk aversion on a team member who, on the contrary, needs positive influence leadership. Fortunately, we have many examples in our study group of people who benefited from a positive influence leader who "saw something" in the person and gave them an assignment where they could blossom.

Coping Strategies for Overcoming Negativity

Our research tells us that many people encounter a negative influence in the course of their life. While many people are beaten down by the forceful negativity of another person, especially an authority figure such as a manager or parent, successful people develop personal mechanisms for coping and, in some cases, thriving as a result of the experience.

In one of the more famous examples of a person overcoming negative influence, evolutionary scientist Charles Darwin was considered by both his family and his early teachers to be a colossal failure. He was asked to leave one of his first schools and dropped out of the University of Edinburg medical college because working on bodies made him sick. At this point his father said to him, "You care for nothing but shooting, dogs, and rat-catching and you are a disgrace to yourself and all your family" (Bland, 2008).

Later, at Cambridge, he found his true north in a course on natural history and, with the positive influence of botanist, John Stevens Henslow, his life and our knowledge of evolution changed forever. After graduation, he joined a five-year voyage around South America where he established his scientific knowledge and research methodology which would eventually result in the publication of the landmark *Origin of Species*.

We have conceptualized five coping strategies:

1. Embrace the Negativity as a Challenge
2. Take Responsibility for the Situation
3. Persevere in the Face of Negativity
4. Adopt a Calm and Reasoned Approach
5. Use the Negativity as a Learning Experience

Embrace the Negativity as a Challenge

Our research indicates that people develop different coping strategies for dealing with negative people in their lives. One approach is to take the negativity as a challenge with an approach that goes something like this: "I'll prove them wrong." We have heard people say, "You think I can't do it; I'll show you" or "You believe my decision makes no sense, you will eat those words."

For example, Jennifer's mother said to her, "What are you going to do with a bachelor's degree? You can't do anything with that." Jennifer then set out to prove her mother wrong and to let her know about it along the way as she moved from intern to a permanent position and on up to chair and curator at the Smithsonian National Museum of American History. Here is how Jennifer puts it:

> I didn't see her (mother) as a negative factor but I did see it as a challenge. On the other hand, Jennifer told us that her mother's passion for history created Jennifer's love of history. Their childhood home was full of history from the furnishings to the paint and down to the last detail.

Gerald, an engineer who had a long, productive career with GE told us about an early negative influence in his life. His high school guidance counselor tried to discourage him when he said he wanted to go to college and study engineering. In fact, when he proposed a double major of engineering and economics, she laughed out loud. He was motivated by the counselor who said to him, "You can't do it." Gerald told us, "It gave me a chip on my shoulder." When questioned, Gerald, an African American, said he did not believe the counselor was a racist. However, she was clearly prejudiced since she had seen few, if any, minorities succeed in this career path. He concluded, "She was just bad at her job."

Jonathan, a senior executive, put it very succinctly: "My mother was always a half empty person. I was motivated to prove her wrong."

Debra, an executive with a pharmaceutical company and a clarinet player, tried out for the University of Michigan Marching Band when she was a freshman. There were only a handful of women in the band at that time. Debra, who is five feet tall, was called up by the director in front of the entire band along with a 6'5" male tuba player who was also a senior and experienced member of the band. Debra told us:

> The band director yelled at me in front of everyone: "He is twice as tall and moves twice as fast." My reaction was abject humiliation and I considered walking away, but then I got mad and said to myself: "I'll show him. He can't make me quit." I worked hard to improve and was voted in as a member of the band.

Debra used the band director's negativity as a motivator. She was determined to prove him wrong.

Take Responsibility for the Situation

Another approach is to tough it out and hope the person will change. Yet another approach, and the one that Nancy took, is to take responsibility for your situation and develop a successful coping strategy. As the human resources (HR) business partner for the chief technology officer (CTO) she quickly realized that he had issues working with senior-level women in the organization. For example, he would rarely meet with Nancy, did not include her in important team meetings, and complained to other senior-level managers that she was incompetent.

Nancy learned that it was possible to work with his organization by forging alliances and partnerships with his team in order to provide the HR services that were needed. One key learning was that she did not need his sponsorship to create many effective working relationships with his team. Another, more powerful learning, was that she was never going to change his assessment of her no matter how great a job she did with his organization. It was his problem! The experience was liberating for Nancy because she learned that she did not need or want to work in an organization that did not value her contributions. She told us, "And that was worth all the stress."

She has now moved on to another organization where she has "always felt supported." In a clear example of "paying it forward," Nancy actively ensures that "No one that I work with ever feels devalued for any reason."

Persevere in the Face of Negativity

Rock and roll icon Elvis Presley overcame an early life that was filled with poverty, rejection, and personal disappointment. He was an average student who, at the age of 10, placed fifth in a singing contest. He was a loner who was often teased by other children. After the family moved to

Memphis, Presley received a C in music in the eighth grade from a teacher who told him he had no aptitude for singing. He continued to play the guitar and sing with little or no success and lots of rejection, including an audition where the band leader told him, "Stick to truck driving because you're never going to make it as a singer."

Presley kept at it, and his big break came when the legendary record producer and owner of the famous Sun Records, Sam Phillips, caught him singing the blues tune "That's All Right." Phillips heard something special in him and immediately taped the song. Within days, it was hit on local radio in Memphis (Wikipedia Contributors, July 21, 2019).

Tony, the martial arts instructor we interviewed, told us of his early experience in the United States Marine Corps pushing for more close-combat training. He wrote articles for USMC publications and gave presentations on the value of such training. Tony finally convinced a forward-looking battalion commander to institute a trial program with the company he was commanding. The program was going well until a new battalion commander arrived who believed the only conditioning that marines needed was long distance running.

Tony made what would be considered a risky move in a military organization, of pushing back on the decision telling the commander, the Commandant of the Marine Corps had said publicly, "We issue Marines combat boots not sneakers." Nevertheless, the close combat training was cancelled to make time for more running. Tony firmly believed in the value of close combat training and continued to push for it. It took some time, but a few years after he left the service, a new Commandant of the Marine Corps, instituted a continuing education program in close combat training vindicating Tony's position. The program exists to this day. Tony's story provides a good example of not letting the negativity of the other person prevent you from pursuing your goal, from being persistent in taking reasonable risks and adopting the position of "I'd rather take a chance and fail, than not try at all."

A similar approach is demonstrated in stories told to us by Barry, a management consultant and executive coach. As a second grader, Barry was entranced with the idea that he could become an artist. He was sketching in pencil, drawing a picture of a hand that Barry remembers being one of the hands from the Sistine Chapel. He was intent on getting it right, so he drew it on tissue paper and from time to time overlaid it on the original.

When he showed it to his teacher, she said he was definitely not an artist and accused him of tracing the hand.

It was years before Barry had the courage to try sketching again. In college he began working in a variety of media and taking some formal classes in art, including drawing. His college teachers told him he not only had a talent for drawing, but for art in general. Later he transferred this talent for art to photography, which has become a life-long passion.

Barry also told us that, as a high school student, he was not much of an athlete, despite trying very hard to succeed at such sports as baseball, basketball, and gymnastics. In that context, he recounted the negative influence of a gymnastics coach who told him in front of the entire class, "Barry, you will never be an athlete."

Barry was not deterred. Later he wanted to learn how to defend himself and thus started taking classes at a karate school. After being at the school for only a few months, a tournament took place. Barry entered the tournament as a white belt or beginner who had no previous fighting experience. He lost decisively but went back for more. His performance impressed some of the black belts who were all ex-military. From this experience, he learned a powerful lesson in dealing with negativity. As Barry put it, "I learned that courage is being afraid of something and doing it anyway. There is always another ounce of effort or another 'wind' I can call on to keep going." Currently, Barry is a sixth-degree black belt with more than forty-five years in martial arts.

Barry's experiences demonstrate yet another style of dealing with a negative influence. His success strategy involves perseverance in the face of negativity, a clear focus on the desired outcome, and the courage to get back up after being knocked down.

Walt Disney, who once famously said, "If you can dream it, you can do it," is another example of facing down rejection and criticism and continuing to persevere. He went bankrupt at age 22, could not pay his rent, and survived by eating dog food. MGM hated *Mickey Mouse* and told him it would never work because a giant mouse would scare women. Distributors rejected *The Three Little Pigs* because it only had four characters, and they felt cartoons should have as many characters as possible. Most of the audience left halfway through a sneak preview of *Snow White and the Seven Dwarfs*.

Disney, who learned from every failure, said, "All the adversity I've had in my life, all my troubles and obstacles, have strengthened me." His story demonstrates that success is the result of perseverance and courage in the face of failure ("How to Keep Believing in Your Dreams Despite Failure: Walt Disney's Story").

Adopt a Calm and Reasoned Approach

At times, the negativity can come wrapped in what might seem like a positive package. Our instructional designer, Beth, had decided to leave her permanent, full-time position to become a free-lance contractor. To leave the company on the best of terms she provided appropriate notice to both her immediate supervisor and the overall manager of the department. The company, in turn, scheduled many rounds of exit interviews in an effort to convince Beth to stay. In the course of those interviews, she shared that she was leaving to start a business and try her hand at consulting.

Her boss was not happy. In fact, he spent a good deal of time trying to convince her that consulting is a risky business and, as she told us, "He said I was making a terrible career move and would regret it." Beth said she appreciated his concern and understood his perspective. In the end he wished me luck but was not really convinced that I was going to be successful. Beth said, "I realized that the move to consulting was risky, but it was the first step to taking control of my career as opposed to waiting for a manager to recognize my dedication and hard work."

Beth's story provides another example of a solid approach to dealing with a negative influence. When the person warns you about the pitfalls of the path you have chosen, remain calm and thank them for their concern. You are not doing this to make a point or prove him wrong. On the other hand, if you feel it might help, take the time to explain why you are choosing this path and that, while you understand the risks, you have a plan to address them. There is no need to burn your bridges.

As Raghunathan (March 19, 2013), points out, if someone...

> ...warns you of the futility of pursuing your dreams, let him know that you feel differently about your chances, or tell her calmly that you would rather take your chances and fail than not try at all. Likewise, if the negative person warns you of the dire consequences of taking what you think is a healthy risk, tell him

> calmly, "we will see what happens." Hopefully, if you have calibrated accurately, you will emerge unhurt, and will enhance your skills. Over time the negative person will recognize that, while your predilection for taking risks may be higher than his or her own, you are not reckless.

Use Negativity as a Learning Experience

Mindi, another person we interviewed, also used working with a negative person as a learning experience. Briefly, she worked on a community project with a boss who was quick to point out all the negatives, fostered competition among the staff, did not listen to or incorporate staff suggestions and rarely provided any encouragement. The negative influence pervaded the environment, stifling inspiration and collaboration among the staff. Mindi watched, learned, and recognized all of the negative qualities she wanted to avoid when she had the opportunity to lead a project. When that opportunity presented itself, Mindi was truly able to blossom and went on to great success as the positive influence leader of a successful community-based project for abused women.

Our sportswriter, Nancy, remembers her high school algebra teacher as a very negative person.

> Early in the year, I was struggling to understand a concept and he was not helpful—at all—just repeatedly telling me to "start at the beginning and figure it out." No actual teaching, no guidance on how I could even go about try to figure it out. My parents eventually asked for a meeting to see what more they or I could be doing. The teacher told my dad that I'd never amount to anything in math. These are pretty crushing words for a 14-year old to hear. (He was well aware I was in the room.)

This experience did not serve as motivation because as Nancy told us, "I'm still awful at math. However, it did make me very cognizant of how I respond to people and the impact my words can have."

Looking Back: Some Issues to Consider

Our experience tells us that negativity can come from a variety of people who we encounter in our life. Sometimes it's a parent who quashes your goal of being a nurse. ("That's a girl's job.") For others it may be a teacher who stomps on your dreams of making the school's honor society. ("You're just not smart enough.") It can be a coach who kills your desire to make the track team. ("You're just too slow and kinda overweight.") Negativity is often in the workplace where you work for a manager who tries to stifle your ambition. ("Don't be so impatient. It took me years to become a supervisor.")

However, as our research shows, successful people develop methods of dealing with these negative forces. They either take it on as a challenge, learn from it, work around the person, or power through it with just a bit more grit. In these situations, many people find it helpful to lean on a mentor, coach, or friend for support, encouragement, and advice as they work through it.

1. Describe a person who tried to impose their negativity on you. What specifically did he or she do? How did you cope?
2. Imagine this conversation early on in your life:

   > *You know it's very tough to break into that field. You have to be very lucky to make it.*

   What would you say?
3. Of the five coping strategies discussed, which is the one you most often used and why?
4. Why are some people like Elvis, Oprah, and Darwin, who get beaten down at an early age, able to persevere and go on to achieve great success?

Chapter 10
The Positive Influence Leader in Times of Crisis

> *So, first of all, let me assert my firm belief that the only thing we have to fear is...fear itself—nameless, unreasoning, unjustified terror which paralyzes needed efforts to convert retreat into advance. In every dark hour of our national life a leadership of frankness and of vigor has met with that understanding and support of the people themselves which is essential to victory. And I am convinced that you will again give that support to leadership in these critical days.*
>
> *More important, a host of unemployed citizens face the grim problem of existence, and an equally great number toil with little return. Only a foolish optimist can deny the dark realities of the moment.*
>
> *Our greatest primary task is to put people to work. This is no unsolvable problem if we face it wisely and courageously.*
>
> *There are many ways in which it can be helped, but it can never be helped merely by talking about it. We must act and act quickly.*
>
> – Franklin Delano Roosevelt
> Inaugural Address, March 3, 1933

Roosevelt's inaugural address is most famous for those words about fear. However, Roosevelt goes on to talk about specific national issues such as unemployment, which, at that time, was at 25 percent. He understands the pain of being unemployed or working but receiving very little for your effort. He's supportive; he gets it, and he is there for the people. However, he also explains that the problems require more than talk; they require concrete solutions, which he will propose to Congress. Roosevelt quickly became a role of positive influence leadership by proposing a series of specific job creating and relief efforts that he had promised in his inaugural address. He walked the talk!

Leadership Challenges of the Coronavirus Crisis of 2020

As we were in the final stages of completing the manuscript for this book, the world was hit with the new coronavirus. It is our view that a crisis of this magnitude requires leadership that is able to adapt to the many challenges faced by organizations during these unprecedented times. Organizations—private, public, and non-profit—and their leaders must be sufficiently agile with an ability to use a leadership style that speaks to the needs of a varied stakeholder group—customers, employees, suppliers, and the public.

We believe this is a time for positive influence leaders who are able to contribute to the success of the organization in a variety of ways.

During a crisis, the effective positive influence leader is:

Supportive: "These are difficult times for all of us, but I am here for you and together we will work to get through it."

A Teacher: "Here is what you need to know and be able to do in order to be successful during this time."

Motivating: "I will encourage you to do what is necessary and I expect you to push back when you think I need to hear something important or need to alter or change course."

A Role Model: "I will try to provide a positive example of how to handle things during this crisis, but you should feel free to develop your own style and methods of getting things done during this time."

The most successful positive influence leaders are situational. They seem to effortlessly alter their style to provide the organization just what is needed at the very time it is needed.

We were encouraged to share our insights during the coronavirus crisis when they could be of help to leaders on the front lines of dealing with the issues arising from the crisis. The result was four articles dealing with various aspects of leadership in a time of crisis:

- In Times of Crisis We Need a Positive Influence Leader
- 5 Ways Real Leaders Act When a Crisis Hits

- When a Crisis Hits, A Transformational Positive Influence Leader Steps Up
- Resist the Rush

In Times of Crisis We Need a Positive Influence Leader

We have all heard a good deal over the years about crisis management. Crisis management often treats a disruption or unexpected event as something to be "managed" in such a way that minimizes harm to the organization. It often begins with denial of or minimizing the event:

- "It's nothing. Don't worry about it."
- "People are exaggerating the situation."
- "It's not that bad."
- "It will all be over soon."

However, in times of a real crisis, such as war, financial meltdown, or pandemic, leadership, not simply management, is required. Real leaders don't deny, deceive, or deflect. We believe, more specifically, in times of crisis that *Positive Influence Leadership* is necessary.

1. **Positive Influence Leaders are Supportive.** They are not cheerleaders who tell everyone that it's going to be fine. They are, however, calm and confident and most of all, truthful. They make it clear that, while this may be a long-term battle, we are in this fight together and "I have your back."

   More specifically, it's a leader like David Gibbs, CEO of Yum Brands (KFC, Pizza Hut, Taco Bell), who just recently made it very clear to their millions of customers and thousands of franchisees around the world that they are "open for business" and well-positioned for this crisis because they long-ago perfected "contactless" delivery, drive-thru, and carry-out.

2. **Positive Influence Leaders are Teachers.** They listen to your concerns. They understand your needs. They provide the information and knowledge you need in order to deal with the crisis. In an attempt to "manage" the crisis, managers often give out confusing and sometimes conflicting information. The most effective positive influence leaders have the knowledge that we all need to get through the crisis and, perhaps more importantly,

they have an ability to communicate that information in a way that we all understand it.

For example, Dr. Deborah Birx, a key member of the White House Coronavirus Task Force and a well-respected global health expert, has what has been described as "that essential and rare skill, which is the ability to explain really complicated, fairly technical, scary health situations in a way that ordinary people can watch the briefings and say, 'I understand, and she's speaking to me.'"

3. **Positive Influence Leaders are Motivators.** They see that something special in you that may not have even been apparent to you. They provide you with the freedom to do your job without micro-managing because they provide a clear statement of the goal and then get out of the way allowing you the freedom to figure out how to get it done. And lastly, they give you access to the resources you need to do the job and empower you to act while making it clear that "I'm here if you need me."

   In that context is Andrew Cuomo, Governor of New York, the epicenter of the virus, who has spoken directly to the people of the state asking that they practice sensible sanitation and limit contact with others, especially in groups because as he said, "We need everyone to be safe, or no one can be safe." He has motivated the state bureaucracy to cooperate, used state labs to get tests done, nudged local officials to close schools and offices, and gotten the military to create more hospital beds to treat virus patients.

4. **Positive Influence Leaders are Role Models.** They can be a powerful force from whom you can learn how to do things "the right way." You can choose to closely emulate a person you admire or you can simply extract certain traits and integrate them with your style. A role model can also be someone you have never met but have admired from afar.

   One such person is Taiwan's Vice President, Chen Chien-jen, an epidemiologist with a doctorate from Johns Hopkins. Under his leadership, back in January when the coronavirus outbreak in neighboring China first became known to the WHO, the country established a national command center to coordinate all government efforts. They quickly began testing patients for coronavirus, established a toll-free number to encourage citizens to report cases, instituted land and sea border controls, active case finding, and quarantine of peopled with suspected infection, and ensuring the health system had the necessary resources to manage patients with the disease.

In a time of crisis—war, financial, or medical—Positive Influence Leadership is essential.

As Abraham Lincoln said a very long time ago:

> *"I am a firm believer in the people. If given the truth, they can be depended upon to meet any national crisis. The great point is to bring them the facts."*

(This article, by Glenn Parker, originally appeared in *CEO World,* April 4, 2020.)

5 Ways Real Leaders Act When a Crisis Hits

> *"How companies respond will define their brand for decades."*
>
> – Mark Cuban

Whether responding to an international, national, local, or company-specific crisis, positive influence role models are a powerful force for showing us how to do things "the right way." They provide an example from which we can learn how to be successful.

You may choose to closely emulate a person you admire; however, you can also benefit by extracting certain traits and integrating them with your unique style.

To be a positive influence role model, follow these five actions:

1. **Be open and authentic.** At the outset of a crisis, you don't want either your customers or your employees to worry, and so there may be a tendency to minimize or sugarcoat the truth. It's also possible that you don't have complete information. However, the worst thing you can do is deny, deceive, or deflect—this opens the door for rumors and distractions.

Be honest and say something like, "This is what we know as of this moment, but the situation is fluid and things may change. However, as soon as I know, you will know."

The textbook case of how to handle a corporate crisis is the 1982 Tylenol tampering episode in which seven people died in Illinois after taking the painkiller. Johnson & Johnson, the maker of Tylenol, relied on its corporate credo that clearly states "Our **first** responsibility is to our patients, doctors and nurses, to mothers and fathers and all others who use our products and services."

As a result, they quickly took responsibility by withdrawing the product from the market, halting further production, and offering to refund or exchange the capsules for solid tablets. Later, it was found that some of the product was poisoned after it reached Chicago and then sold to unsuspecting customers. In the end, Johnson & Johnson, and specifically CEO James Burke, was applauded for their quick and candid response to the crisis. As a result, Tylenol ultimately regained most of its previous market share.

Transparency builds trust and loyalty. Trust is the cornerstone of authenticity, a hallmark of the positive influence role model leader. People—both employees and customers—will follow you if they see you as the real deal.

2. **Be clear and specific.** In the current coronavirus crisis, Dr. Anthony Fauci has become familiar to millions of Americans and is universally seen as a calm and constant voice of reason. Dr. Fauci, director of the National Institute of Allergy and Infectious Diseases (NIAID) has been involved in every epidemic in the past 40 years, including HIV/AIDS and Ebola. However, it is his ability to clearly explain complex scientific and arcane medical issues and make them easily understood by the general public that has made him a great example of a positive influence role model leader.

   Your colleagues and employees are listening closely to what you say and how you say it. Avoid minimizing a situation or being overly optimistic. Speak your truth clearly and specifically. As Mark Twain once said, "Tell the truth and you never have to remember anything."

3. **Listen, Ask Questions, Listen Some More, and Respond.** During a crisis (and in normal times, as well) positive influence role models are open and accessible to their team—and they listen. They listen to their concerns both technical and emotional.

   Many companies are holding regular all-hands videoconference meetings where employees can ask questions and discuss their concerns about how to balance work-family issues during the crisis. A few organizations are also ending the week with a virtual happy hour where team members can share lighthearted stories about their work-at-home experiences.

   Leaders who listen also learn ideas from employees on how to work smarter and create work processes that increase efficiency and effectiveness. When leaders are open and accessible, employees eagerly provide insights into both the degree and elements of customer satisfaction.

   The most effective positive influence role models not only listen, but they respond with plans to implement these ideas. As a result, companies with a culture of positive influence role models typically emerge from a crisis in a much stronger position.

4. **Walk the talk.** Role models or, more specifically, the most successful positive influence roles models are well aware that people are watching. In this context it is axiomatic that if, for example, you want members of your team to provide extraordinary customer service during a crisis (and beyond) then all of **your** customer interactions must meet or exceed that same elevated standard.

   Leaders at the top of the house can set the standard by being a role model who walks the talk. Such was the more recent case of Kevin Johnson, Starbucks CEO, when he found the company in the eye of a negative storm because two African American men were arrested in one of their shops in Philadelphia for no apparent reason. Relying on the company's top corporate value of "creating a culture of warmth and belonging where everyone is welcome," Johnson quickly apologized to the men and to the nation. Within a week, Starbucks announced that it would close all of its 8,000 stores for an afternoon to provide staff training on implicit bias and ways of ensuring that everyone feels safe and welcome in their stores.

Values statements look good framed and hung in corporate conference rooms, but they only come alive when customers and employees see you "live those values" through your actions. In other words, when you walk the talk.

5. **Conduct an after-action review.** When the crisis is over, there is a strong tendency to quickly get back to business as usual or the way things were before the crisis. However, the most effective positive influence leaders take some time to review and learn from the experience. You can call it an evaluation session, an assessment, or the more formal after-action review. The simple facts are:

    - There may be another crisis in the future and you would like to learn how to handle it better.
    - It is quite possible that things have changed as a result of the crisis and it is not possible to return to business as usual. For example, some customers are no longer able to willing to buy your product or service.
    - You may have done some new things during the crisis that you now want to integrate into regular business operations going forward. For example, you find that video conferencing works well for many meetings and, therefore, you will reduce or eliminate a large number of face-to-face meetings.

    You may use different language, but most project reviews focus on:

    - What was our goal(s)?
    - What happened/what did we do?
    - What worked? Why?
    - What didn't work? Why?
    - What should we do differently next time?

    In times of crisis, the effective positive influence role model leader can be a powerful force who encourages you to think outside of the box and not limit your options to the conventional ways of doing things or past practices. During this period, they are open, honest, clear, and specific. They do not sugarcoat the harsh realities of the situation, but they also create a participatory process that includes lots of questions and an equal amount of listening. Perhaps most important, they "walk the talk" and thus ensure their actions are always consistent with their words.

(A slightly edited version of this article by Glenn Parker appeared in *Real Leaders,* April 19, 2020.)

When a Crisis Hits, a Transformational Positive Influence Leader Steps Up

When a crisis hits, we need leaders with different talents and styles to be positive influences on the organization.

- We need smart leaders who quickly master complex information, communicate it in terms easily understood, and then are able to make it work to the benefit of the organization.
- We need skilled leaders who can effectively communicate with large groups of people using modern communications technology.
- We need analytical leaders who can quickly and accurately prioritize problems, mission-critical goals, tasks, and expenses.
- We need supportive leaders who can listen, empathize, and articulate the emotions and stress felt by employees, customers, and suppliers and then respond with a plan of action.
- We need authentic leaders who are open and confident role models but who also get things done.

During our research for *Positive Influence: The Leader Who Helps People Become Their Best Self,* we found that there are four styles of positive influence leader, all of whom can contribute to the success of an organization, but in different ways. A positive influence leader is supportive, an exceptional teacher, motivating, and a confident role model. A transformational leader effortlessly alters their approach to provide just what the organization needs at the very time it is needed. They are situational.

The Supportive Positive Influence Leader. Many positive influence leaders are especially effective in communicating in an open and honest manner with employees and customers that "although things are tough now, I am here to support you for the duration of this crisis." However, they also provide an honest assessment of the situation without minimizing or sugarcoating things. In a crisis that involves some scary health and safety issues, the leader must make it abundantly clear that employee health is our number one concern over and above short-term profits and shareholder value.

Mark Cuban, owner of the Dallas Mavericks NBA basketball team, is an excellent example of supportive positive influence leadership. When the NBA announced it was suspending the season due to the virus, one the first things that Cuban did was make it clear that all arena workers—ticket takers, food and drink stand employees, maintenance staff—would be paid even if there were no games. Beyond that, Cuban has made it clear to other CEOs that "by doing right by your employees, you do more to help stabilize the economy and from there, we have a better chance of getting back to business as usual." Cuban believes that consumers, especially young people, will remember how you acted during the crisis and make their future buying decisions based on that. Many people also want to work for an organization that cares about the community in which they live.

The supportive positive influence leader believes in their people, but perhaps more importantly, helps the people believe in themselves.

The Teacher Positive Influence Leader. Crisis situations often involve complex technical, scientific, financial, and other similar issues that may be difficult to master, especially when under stress. The teacher leader is a positive influence in a crisis because they help you comprehend your situation by explaining things in terms you can understand. Clarity is especially important because being acutely aware of your situation can reduce your anxiety and increase your ability to take concrete actions. The most effective positive influence teachers do something more than teach. They awaken in you an active desire to learn, to develop your skills and knowledge to be your best self. You want to take responsibility for your personal development so you can better understand the crisis and take appropriate action.

There is no better example of a teacher positive influence leader than Dr. Anthony Fauci, the *de facto* leader of the White House Coronavirus Task Force. While he is the world's leading expert on infectious diseases, it is his extraordinary ability to explain complicated medical issues in terms that the rest of us can understand that is his special skill. He is the gold standard in the world of public health, and yet he still seems like good old Uncle Tony explaining to the kids how to throw a curve ball in the back yard after a family dinner. The White House is taking advantage of Dr. Fauci's communications skills using social media to reach young people via Instagram, YouTube, and podcasts such as "Pardon My Take."

The Motivating Positive Influence Leader. A crisis calls for a special variety of leadership. When disaster strikes, some people deny its existence, some get paralyzed with fear, some engage in risky behavior to show how tough they are, and others wait to be told what to do. The most effective motivating leader inspires, pushes, or perhaps pulls you to take the necessary actions. If you fail, she will pick you back up, help you learn from your mistakes (while admitting her mistakes, too) and get you to see that success is still very much possible. The effective positive influence leader is not necessarily a motivational speaker, but rather a solid, practical, results-oriented person who will tell you what you need to hear and get you moving in the right direction.

One such person is Gina Raimondo, governor of Rhode Island, who got into a public squabble with Governor Cuomo of New York when she instituted a policy of stopping all cars with New York plates at the state border and requiring others who planned to stay in the state to quarantine themselves for 14 days. She later amended the order to apply to all out-of-state drivers. Governor Raimondo acted on the belief that her first responsibility is to protect the citizens of her state. Positive influence leaders like the governor are calm and clear and willing to change course as warranted by the facts. For example, at first when tests were scarce, she strongly discouraged people with mild symptoms from seeking a test. Just recently, when the state was able to test some 1,000 people per day, she said, "I am telling you something different now. I don't want you to be shy about coming forward if you think you have coronavirus symptoms."

The Role Model Positive Influence Leader. A positive influence role model can be a powerful force in an organization and in your life. They provide an example of how to be a successful leader, especially in a time of crisis. You can choose to closely emulate the person, or you may elect to integrate some of their strengths while maintaining your unique style. For many people, their role model is someone they have never met but admired from afar. They learn by observing the person and researching how they handle various situations.

Prior to the coronavirus outbreak, few people outside of the army knew about Lt. Gen. Todd Semonite who has become a key leader in the fight against the virus and a role model to many. Semonite is the commander of the Army Corps of Engineers and leader of the mobilization to quickly build temporary hospitals to treat both COVID-19 and non-COVID-19 patients by converting existing convention centers, dorms, and hotels. In the rapidly evolving situation, he has demonstrated the very best in teamwork and collaboration by working seamlessly with federal agencies such as FEMA, HHS, and Defense as well as governors, mayors, and the White House Task Force.

The Transformational Positive Influence Leader. The transformational positive influence leader is equally comfortable and skilled at using any one of the four styles as dictated by the needs of the crisis. In addition, he is able to assess your needs at the moment and seamlessly adapt and alter his approach to provide just what you need and in a way that you can use it. In other words, he is situational.

The transformational leader modifies their approach based on the situation and the needs of the people in their organization. At times he can be supportive ("you got this"), at other times, a teacher ("here are the facts as we know them now"), on occasion motivating ("this is your moment") and, when necessary, a role model ("this is what I said we would do").

Who is that transformational positive influence leader in this crisis? People who have been "nominated" include:

- Andrew Cuomo, Governor of New York
- Mark Cuban, Owner of the Dallas Mavericks and Entrepreneur
- Chuck robbins, CEO of Cisco Systems
- Dr. Deborah Birx, White House Task Force on the Virus
- Gretchen Whitmer, Governor or Michigan
- Gavin Newsome, Governor of California
- David Gibbs, CEO of Yum Brands (KFC, Pizza Hut, Taco Bell)
- The people profiled in this article
- Please nominate other leaders

Who is your choice? How can you incorporate the traits each of these positive influence leaders possess into your leadership style?

(This article, by Glenn Parker, originally appeared in *Smart Brief,* April 30, 2020.)

Resist the Rush

At some point, the coronavirus crisis will be over. Social distancing will be a thing of the past. Group meetings will be pronounced safe. Businesses will reopen. Most people will be happy and eager to get back to work. Learning and development activities will begin, once again, to ramp up. Hold on. Just as we stop those who rush out of the room after a class before taking time to complete the program evaluation form or post-test, it's important to push back against the urge to quickly get back to business as usual.

It is quite possible the organization has been permanently changed by this crisis—returning to ways of old may not be possible. Perhaps a key customer or supplier is no longer in business or most teams have adopted new work practices, such as videoconferencing.

As organizations return to work, they will need to evaluate what worked and what did not because there will be another crisis in the future—it may not be health related and it may not be of the same scale, but it will need to be addressed so the organization is better prepared to meet its challenges.

Call it an assessment, an evaluation, or an after-action review, but organizational development (OD) and training professionals can be positive influence leaders by encouraging people to think outside the box and resist conventional ways of doing things. These positive influence leaders can guide teams at all levels of the organization with key questions coupled with a positive process designed to facilitate the development of a proactive plan for the future.

Key Review Questions:

- What was our goal during the time/what did we hope to achieve?
- What actually happened/what did we do?
- What changed over the course of time?
- What worked well? What didn't work well/what could have gone better?
- What should we do differently next time?
- What are some key lessons learned that can be applied in future crisis situations?

- What things worked well during this time that we should incorporate in the way we work in the future?
- What personal lessons did you learn from this experience?

Key Process Elements:

- **Preparation**
  - Set a time limit for the session (e.g., 2 hours or half day).
  - Prepare questions in advance for display in the room.
  - The questions may also be sent to the participants in advance of the session.
  - Consider using a scribe to take notes on the conclusions and recommendations.
- **Meeting Facilitation**
  - Use a professional OD or training facilitator to manage the process.
  - The facilitator should use open-ended questions to engage the participants.
  - If participation is limited to a few people, encourage each person to share, at a minimum, one thing that worked and one that did not.
- **Summary and Recommendations**
  - Ensure that you leave enough time to summarize the conclusions and action items for the future.
  - Focus the conclusions on specific actionable recommendations; e.g., "at the beginning, set up an organization-wide coordination committee."
  - Ask for feedback on the value of the review experience.
  - Thank everyone for their participation.
  - Send everyone a meeting summary.

As a crisis comes to an end, training and OD professionals can be positive influence leaders by helping organizations learn from the experience and develop strategies for coping with similar challenges that may arise in the future, as well as integrating learnings from the experience into the near-term workplace.

(This article, by Glenn Parker, originally appeared in *TRAINING Magazine*, April 29, 2020.)

Looking Back: Some Issues to Consider

There will be another crisis. Hopefully, it will not be as severe as the coronavirus. For an organization, that crisis may be a security breech, a product recall, a major customer complaint, a supply chain breakdown, or a public relations gaff. In such cases and others, positive influence leaders must be prepared to step up and take responsibility for addressing the issue and developing a plan of action.

1. During a crisis, which of the four styles is likely to be most effective?
2. Embedded corporate values often provide the basis for a leader's response to a crisis.
    - What values of your organization would be most useful during a crisis?
3. The teacher positive influence leader is someone who is able to break down complex issues and make them easily understood by everyone in the organization.
    - Why types of crises most need leaders who can explain things to you while also motivating you to learn more about the issue.
4. In the desire to get back to "normal" quickly, we often forget or decide to forgo a project review.
    - What is your experience with after-action reviews?
    - What would be the value of an after-action review following a crisis for your organization?

Part 4

Tools for the Positive Influence Leader

The Parker Positive Influence Leader Survey: A Self-Assessment

Purpose

The Parker Positive Influence Leader Survey will help you to identify your leadership style, assess your current strengths, and create a plan for increasing your effectiveness as a positive leadership influence person.

Directions: Please answer each statement by indicating how you act *now* rather than how you would like to function in the future. This is a survey, not a test. Therefore, there are no right or wrong answers.

Answer each of the eighteen sentences. Each of the following 18 questions has four choices. Rank the choice in the space provided using the following scale:

4 – Most Like Me
3 – Somewhat Like Me
2 – Somewhat Unlike Me
1 – Least Like Me

For accurate scoring of your results, be sure to assign only one rank—1, 2, 3, or 4—to each option. Do not make ties.

The Parker Positive Influence Leader Survey

1. As a leader of a team, I see my principal role as: (**Rank** 1, 2, 3, or 4)
   ____ a. believing in the ability of team members to get the job done.
   ____ b. inspiring people on the team to use their skills to achieve great things.
   ____ c. being an advocate for members of the team.
   ____ d. being a role model they can emulate.

2. When I see that someone in my organization is struggling to find their way, I: (**Rank** 1, 2, 3, or 4)
   ____ a. teach them what they need to know to get back on track.
   ____ b. help them see their lack of focus and suggest possible alternatives.
   ____ c. share my experience in dealing with similar situations.
   ____ d. make it clear that I am behind them all the way.

3. Usually people see me as a: (**Rank** 1, 2, 3, or 4)
   ____ a. motivator.
   ____ b. positive example.
   ____ c. supportive person.
   ____ d. inspiring teacher.

4. I believe effective leadership requires: (**Rank** 1, 2, 3, or 4)
   ____ a. sharing your vision of the path forward.
   ____ b. fostering a "can-do" mentality
   ____ c. creating a desire to be the best.
   ____ d. putting people in a position to be successful.

5. At times I can also be: (**Rank** 1, 2, 3, or 4)
   ____ a. unrealistic in my assessment of people.
   ____ b. unaware of what people really need from me.
   ____ c. quick to do it for the person rather than teach them to do it.
   ____ d. too remote and inaccessible to people.

6. As a mentor, my goal is to: (**Rank** 1, 2, 3, or 4)
   ____ a. teach the person things they need to learn in order to be successful.
   ____ b. help the person find their true north; their true calling.
   ____ c. be a positive example from whom the person can learn.
   ____ d. encourage the person to believe they can do it.

7. During team meetings, I usually: (**Rank** 1, 2, 3, or 4)
   ____ a. provide team members with problem-solving tools rather than solve the problem for them.
   ____ b. trust the process that the team has seen me use will help them to reach the best decision.
   ____ c. provide positive reinforcement to members of the team.
   ____ d. ensure that team members have sufficient information about the issues.

8. When necessary, I am able to: (**Rank** 1, 2, 3, or 4)
   ____ a. push people beyond their perceived limits.
   ____ b. be tough but caring.
   ____ c. share the harsh realities of the world.
   ____ d. provide direct and honest feedback.

9. When things go wrong, I usually: (**Rank** 1, 2, 3, or 4)
   ____ a. make it clear that success is still possible.
   ____ b. provide the knowledge or skills needed to get back on track.
   ____ c. help people learn from their mistakes and move forward.
   ____ d. provide an example where corrective action produced a positive outcome.

10. I see the role of the coach as: (**Rank** 1, 2, 3, or 4)
   ____ a. helping a person learn what they need to be successful.
   ____ b. not allowing the person to settle for second best.
   ____ c. ensuring that my actions are consistent with my words.
   ____ d. getting a person to believe in themselves.

11. I believe team problem-solving requires: (**Rank** 1, 2, 3, or 4)
    ____ a. a process that includes direct and honest communication.
    ____ b. a leader who demonstrates a positive work ethic.
    ____ c. a culture where members are supportive of each other.
    ____ d. an environment where members are open to learn from each other.

12. As a member of a team, I can be most effective by: (**Rank** 1, 2, 3, or 4)
    ____ a. being a positive example for others on the team.
    ____ b. supporting other team members when they ask for help.
    ____ c. teaching my co-workers things they need to learn.
    ____ d. bringing out the best in other members of my team.

13. At times I make others uncomfortable because I: (**Rank** 1, 2, 3, or 4)
    ____ a. appear to be so positive most of the time.
    ____ b. believe in them even when they don't believe in themselves.
    ____ c. believe that failure is a necessary step in learning to be successful.
    ____ d. seem to perform at a level they think they will never achieve.

14. I believe the role of a leader is to: (**Rank** 1, 2, 3, or 4)
    ____ a. provide people with the tools they need to succeed.
    ____ b. help people recognize and make the most effective use of their strengths.
    ____ c. articulate the change in a way that others will want to follow.
    ____ d. help people see that what seems impossible is possible.

15. Most of the time I am: (**Rank** 1, 2, 3, or 4)
    ____ a. willing to help but not do it for you.
    ____ b. a person from whom you can learn what it takes to succeed.
    ____ c. insistent on doing things the right way.
    ____ d. willing to help you learn better ways of doing things.

16. I believe the best team decisions are made in: (**Rank** 1, 2, 3, or 4)
    ____ a. a meeting where the leader models a participative process.
    ____ b. a supportive and positive environment.
    ____ c. an atmosphere where people respect the knowledge and skills of their teammates.
    ____ d. a culture where the leader surfaces and utilizes the strengths of people.

17. An effective teacher is someone who: (**Rank** 1, 2, 3, or 4)
    ____ a. believes that everyone is capable of learning.
    ____ b. creates a desire in people to increase their knowledge and skills.
    ____ c. often sees strengths in people that were not apparent to them.
    ____ d. people often see as someone they seek to emulate.

18. Sometimes I become impatient with a person who: (**Rank** 1, 2, 3, or 4)
    ____ a. refuses to acknowledge the things they need to learn to be successful
    ____ b. I see as having strengths that they refuse to accept.
    ____ c. attempts to mimic my approach rather than adapting it to their unique life and work style.
    ____ d. I believe in but who does not believe in themselves.

Scoring Your Results

Directions: In the chart on the next page, record your answers for questions 1 through 18 in the appropriate boxes.

Be careful when recording the numbers. The order of the letters changes for each question. For example, for question 1 the order is a, b, c, d, but for question 2 the order is d, a, b, c.

The sum of the four totals must equal 180.

Please continue to the next page to record your results.

Survey Results

Question	SL	TL	ML	RML
1	a.	b.	c.	d.
2	d.	a.	b.	c.
3	c.	d.	a.	b.
4	b.	c.	d.	a.
5	a.	b.	c.	d.
6	d.	a.	b.	c.
7	c.	d.	a.	b.
8	b.	c.	d.	a.
9	a.	b.	c.	d.
10	d.	a.	b.	c.
11	c.	d.	a.	b.
12	b.	c.	d.	a.
13	a.	b.	c.	d.
14	d.	a.	b.	c.
15	c.	d.	a.	b.
16	b.	c.	d.	a.
17	a.	b.	c.	d.
18	d.	a.	b.	c.
TOTALS →				

The highest number in the bottom row refers to your **Primary Positive Influence Leader Style.** If there are two or more numbers that are within three points of each other, then all of them are your primary leader style. The lowest total is called your **Least Active Positive Influence Leader Style.**

Your **Primary Positive Influence Leader Style** incorporates a group of behaviors that you use most often as a leader. However, this style is not necessarily the only style you use. Each of us has the capacity to use any one of the four styles. We simply use one style—our primary style—most often.

Understanding Your Results

SL = SUPPORTIVE LEADER

If you are a supportive leader, you do your best to help people believe in themselves and believe in their ability to overcome any challenge that comes their way. You foster a "can-do" feeling among the people you manage while making it clear that they can count on you to stand with them. As required, you provide people in your unit with positive reinforcement, although, at times, you may not be aware just what a person needs from you. The supportive leader may not always teach people the needed values and skills or create a work culture where team members make effective use of their strengths.

TL = TEACHER LEADER

If you are a teacher leader, you focus on teaching people the things they need to learn in order to be successful. You create a learning environment on your team where people want to increase their skills and knowledge. However, you also foster a need to absorb a positive value system—that there is a right way to do things and it may not always be the easiest way. While you are always ready to help people acquire the skills and knowledge they need, you can become impatient with people who think they already know enough to be successful. The teacher leader often does not spend enough time getting people to believe in themselves or recognize that people frequently need a positive example to learn from and emulate.

ML = MOTIVATING LEADER

If you are motivating leader, you inspire people to find their true purpose in life. You are often the first person to see positive attributes in people on your team that they were unaware they possessed. As a result, you are most willing to be an advocate for your people, to position them to be successful, and provide them with the necessary tools while empowering them to use those tools to make important decisions. While you are usually inclined to believe in your people, you sometimes become annoyed when a member of your team is unable to acknowledge or use their strengths or see that a mistake is a necessary step in the process of learning to be successful. At times, the motivating leader may not realize that people in their organization closely study their actions to learn the keys to success and recognize that some need to hear that the leader supports and believes in them.

RML = ROLE MODEL LEADER

If you are a role model leader, you understand that at all times your actions must be completely aligned with your words—as the saying goes, you need to "walk the talk." You are aware that people look up to you, not only for guidance but for the right way to do things. You see your role as providing the team with a clear vision of the path forward, a strategy that has a reasonable chance of success, and a process that holds everyone to the highest standards. While you want people on your team to learn from your example, sometimes they see you as remote and operating at such an elevated level that they feel is impossible for them to attain. The role model leader may, at times, forget that people may first need help finding their true north as well as learning the values or skills needed to achieve a successful work life.

Tools for Becoming a More Effective Positive Influence Leader

1. **Build on Your Strengths.** You can be an effective leader using any one of these four styles. Seek out ways to increase the strengths of your primary positive influence leader style.
2. **Expand Your Repertoire.** Plan to incorporate the strengths of some of the other styles. For example, if you are a role model leader, look to increase your ability to be a supportive influence on people.
3. **Seek out Work Environments Where Your Strengths Can Be Utilized.** For example, as a motivating leader, you might look for work culture where people need an inspiring leader who can articulate a clear purpose and bring out the best in them.
4. **Understand the Possibility of Becoming an Ineffective Positive Influence Leader.** Study your survey results, talk to some colleagues about your potential for either using your strengths to an excess (e.g., unrealistically positive about some people) or not using the strengths of your least active styles when situations demand it. You may elect to ask colleagues to complete a companion version of this survey to collect more specific feedback data (360° feedback) on your strengths and areas of potential improvement.

My Improvement Plan

Process: Use this form to begin the process of increasing your effectiveness as a positive influence leader. After you have completed the form, discuss it with a trusted colleague and incorporate their feedback.

Strengths: I see my strengths as:

- ______________________________
- ______________________________
- ______________________________
- ______________________________

On-the-Job Application: I use my strengths in the following situations/ following ways:

- ______________________________
- ______________________________
- ______________________________
- ______________________________

Potential for Ineffectiveness: My tendencies to become an ineffective leader are:

- ______________________________
- ______________________________
- ______________________________
- ______________________________

Improvement Plan: I can be a more effective positive influence leader by:

- ______________________________
- ______________________________
- ______________________________
- ______________________________

References

Abdul-Jabbar, Kareem, *Coach Wooden and Me: Our 50-Year Relationship On and Off the Court*. New York: Grand Central Publishing, 2017.

Adams, Jonathan, "Tyneeda Rivers, Mikal Bridges' Mom: Five Fast Facts You Need to Know," June 21, 2018. Retrieved from: *https://heavy.com/sports/2018/06/mikal-bridges-mom-sixers-tyneeha-rivers/*

Bland, Archie, "The Big Question: How Important was Charles Darwin, and What is His Legacy Today?" December 30, 2008. Retrieved from: *https://www.independent.co.uk/news/science/the-big-question-how-important-was-charles-darwin-and-what-is-his-legacy-today-1216258.html.*

Bromberg, Lila, "Vonn Works to Empower Young Girls," USA TODAY, Monday, August 19, 2019, p. 5C.

Bryant, Adam, "The Power of Following Your Instincts." *Corner Office, The New York Times*, Sunday, May 28, 2017.

Callaway, Julia, "The Language and Influences of the Early Bob Dylan," May 13, 2013. Retrieved from: *https://blog.oxforddictionaries.com/2013/05/24/bob-dylan*.

Carmody, Diedre, "Feminists Shifting Emphasis from Persons to Politics," *New York Times*, August 22, 1972. Retrieved from: *https://www.nytimes.com/1972/08/22/archives/feminists-shifting-emphasis-from-persons-to-politics-feminists-are.html.*

Coffey, Wayne, "Pioneer Gibson Gets Due Credit," USA TODAY, Tuesday, August 27, 2019. P. 3C.

Cook, Sarah and Steve Macaulay, "Making a Difference," *Training Journal*, April, 2014. Retrieved from: *https://www.trainingjournal.com/articles/feature/making-difference.*

Covey, Stephen R., "First, Be Influenced," *Executive Excellence*, Vol. 12, Iss. 1, Jan. 1995, p. 3.

Coyne, Kate, "Melissa McCarthy: My Life Right Now," May 21, 2018. Retrieved from: *https://www.scribd.com/article/378956550/Melissa-Mc-Carthy-I-Love-My-Life-Right-Now*

Entis, Laura, "5 Famous Business Leaders on the Power of Mentorship," August 6, 2015. Retrieved from: *https://www.entrepreneur.com/slideshow/249233*.

Fradkin, Lori, "These Successful Women Prove the Power of a Role Model." December 6, 2017. Retrieved from: *https://www.huffpost.com/entry/famous-role-models-women_n_3915845*.

Franklin, Benjamin, *Autobiography*. New York: Macmillan, 2017.

George, Bill, *Discover Your True North.* Hoboken, NJ: John Wiley, 2015.

"How to Keep Believing in Your Dreams Despite Failure: Walt Disney's Story." (September 3, 2017). Retrieved from*: https://onelifeandyou.com/overcome-failure-keep-believing-dreams-walt-disneys-story/*.

Igoe, Katherine J., "John David Washington and Dad Denzel Washington Are a Father-Son Dream Team." Feb 24, 2019. Retrieved from: *https://www.marieclaire.com/celebrity/a26409685/denzel-washington-john-david-washington/*

Jensen, Erik, "Everything Oprah in One Place," *USA Today*, June 8, 2018, Page 3D.

Kaufman Sarah L., "How Chita Rivera Keeps Dancing at 83, with 16 Screws in Her Leg," *Washington Post*, May 26, 2018.

Luft, Joseph and Harrington Ingham, "The Johari Window: A Graphic Model of Interpersonal Awareness." *Proceedings of the Western Training Laboratory in Group Development*. Los Angeles: University of California, 1955.

Ma, Julia, "25 Famous Women on Their Mentors." January 26, 2017. Retrieved from: *https://www.thecut.com/2017/01/25-famous-women-on-their-mentors.html*.

Mancoff, Deborah, "Vincent Van Gogh's Biography." Retrieved from: *https://entertainment.howstuffworks.com/arts/artwork/vincent-van-gogh-biography3.htm*

McFadden, Katie, "Dominique Dawes, First American Gold Medal Olympic Gymnast, is 'Thrilled' for Gabby Douglas," *Travelers Today*, August 3, 2012. Retrieved from: *https://www.travelerstoday.com/articles/2561/20120803/dominique-dawes-first-african-american-gold-*